IBN KHAFIF (D. 371)

CORRECT ISLAMIC DOCTRINE

(AL-AQÎDA AL-SAHÎHA)

Translation and Notes by
Gibril Fouad Haddad

Damascus
1998

بِسْمِ اللهِ الرَّحْمٰنِ الرَّحِيمِ

وَصَلَّى اللهُ عَلَى سَيِّدِنَا مُحَمَّدٍ وَعَلَى آلِه وَصَحْبِه وَسَلَّم

رَبِّ يَسِّرْ وَلَا تُعَسِّرْ

This work is humbly dedicated to

**Mawlana al-Shaykh Muhammad Nazim Adil
al-Qubrusi al-Naqshbandi al-Haqqani,**

to Shaykh Muhammad Hisham Kabbani,
and to their friends and followers worldwide.

"The pivot of works is correct doctrine and good principles."
AL-QARI, *SHARH MUSNAD ABI HANIFA.*

As-Sunna Foundation of America is an affiliate of the Islamic Supreme Council of America. The Islamic Supreme Council of America is a non-profit, non-governmental organization dedicated to working for the cause of Islam on a bilateral level. As an affiliate of ISCA, ASFA strives to promote unity among Muslims and understanding and awareness about mainstream Islam through education. Its focus is on publishing works that support traditional, accepted approaches to Islamic jurisprudence and law.

ISBN: 95-930409-01-X

Published by:
As-Sunna Foundation of America
2415 Owen Rd Ste B
Fenton, MI 48430
email: asfa@sunnah.org

www.sunnah.org
www.islamicsupremecouncil.org

Foreword

Bismillahir-Rahmanir-Raheem

All praise is due to Allah Almighty who has revived in the hearts of His servants thirst for understanding the Islamic doctrine, *al-'aqeedah.* Blessings and salutations on His Beloved Servant Muhammad 🕮, whom He raised to the station of nearness and whom he blessed with the revelation of Divine Guidance.

As-Sunna Foundation of America is honored to make available to the reading public this new set of translations of classical Islamic texts – the *Islamic Doctrines and Beliefs* series. We congratulate Dr. Gabriel Haddad for his efforts in bringing these outstanding classical manuscripts to light in the English language, as these books are a necessity for every Muslim home, school, library and university.

These works have reached us through distant centuries, authored by scholars who spent the whole of their lives in devotion to Allah and to spreading the knowledge of His great religion. They will undoubtedly stand witness for their authors on the Day of Judgment, wherein *"Whoever works righteousness benefits his own soul"* [41: 46], for every drop of blood running in the veins of such pious and sincere sages was infused with their intense devotion to preserve the fundamentals and the branches of Islam. Reliance on classical texts such as these by the sages Muhammad ibn Khafif ibn Asfakshad and Shaykh Muhyi al-Din Ibn 'Arabi leaves little room for the introduction of alien creeds or uneducated speculation. Due to the extravagant efforts scholars made to compile these books, they are comprehensible and applicable to the general reader and student of religion.

Likewise the efforts of Dr. Haddad, who spent long days and nights in perfecting these translations, is something that we pray will be highly rewarded in this life and the next, for his intention and ours is to broadcast and clarify the pure and unadulterated teachings of *Ahl as-Sunna wal-Jama'a,* The People of the Sunnah and the Majority, whose foundations were laid by the Prophet 🕮 under the direction of his Lord, whose walls were erected by the *Salaf as-saliheen,* the pious predecessors, and whose roof and domes were built by the *Khalaf as-sadiqeen,* the truthful successors up to the present age.

The Importance of Knowledge of Correct *'Aqeedah*

Due to the fact that every generation witnesses a silent decline in worshippers' knowledge of the fundamental doctrines and beliefs of religion, constant efforts are required to elucidate and preserve the sources of this knowledge and to preserve them in the hearts and minds of Allah's servants. The acquisition of knowledge is obligatory for every accountable Muslim, for without it the appearance of conjecture and uneducated opinion is inevitable. Therein lies a danger that leads to an erroneous understanding of faith, which if left unchecked, may lead the seeker to a dangerous precipice from which he is unable to escape a serious fall.

The correct understanding of the signs of Allah Almighty, His Angels, His Books, His Prophets, the Day of Judgment, and the Divine Decree saves one from two extremes: denial of Allah's attributes, and its opposite anthropomorphism, the relating of Allah's attributes to physical manifestations.

There is no time better than today to introduce these books to those for whom English is the mother tongue, for the subject of 'aqeedah has become one of controversy and confusion. These books provide a classical approach to understanding Islamic doctrine, based on some of the most accepted and reliable scholars of *Ahl as-Sunnah wal-Jama'ah*, the Saved Group.

Praise be to Allah, Lord of the Worlds, and salutations and blessings of peace on His Perfect Servant, Muhammad 竮.

Shaykh Muhammad Hisham Kabbani
1 Ramadan, 1420
December 8, 1999
Fenton, Michigan, USA

Contents

About Ibn Khafif (276?-371)

Ibn Khafif is Muhammad ibn Khafif ibn Asfakshad, Abu 'Abd Allah al-Shirazi al-Dibbi al-Shafi'i al-Sufi. Al-Sulami said of him: "The Folk *(al-qawm,* i.e. the Sufis) do not have anyone older than him nor more complete in his state and reality today." He once said: "If you hear the call to prayer and do not see me in the first row, look for me in the cemetaries." He took *kalâm* from Imam Abu al-Hasan al-Ash'ari, *fiqh* from Ibn Surayj, and *tasawwuf* from Ruwaym, al-Jariri, and Abu al-'Abbas ibn 'Ata'. Al-Dhahabi said of him: "He is at the same time one of the most knowledgeable shaykhs in the external sciences *('ulûm al-zâhir).*" Ibn Taymiyya names him among the great Sufi representatives of the Sunna:

> The great shaykhs mentioned by Abu 'Abd al-Rahman al-Sulami in *Tabaqat al-Sufiyya* and Abu al-Qasim al-Qushayri in *al-Risala* were adherents of the school of *Ahl al-Sunna wa al-Jama'a* and the school of *Ahl al-Hadith*, such as Fudayl ibn 'Iyad, al-Junayd ibn Muhammad, Sahl ibn 'Abd Allah al-Tustari, 'Amr ibn 'Uthman al-Makki, Abu 'Abd Allah Muhammad ibn Khafif al-Shirazi, and others, and their speech is found in the Sunna, and they composed books about the Sunna.[1]

Ibn Khafif reported from his teacher Ibn Surayj that the proof that love of Allah was a categorical obligation *(fard)* was in the verses: **❨Say: If your fathers, and your sons, and your brethren, and your wives, and your tribe, and the wealth you have acquired, and merchandise for which you fear that there will be no sale, and dwellings you desire are dearer to you than Allah and His messenger and striving in His way: then wait till Allah brings His command to pass. Allah guides not wrongdoing folk.❩** (9:24) For punishment is not threatened except due to a categorical obligation.

Ibn Khafif disapproved of the flight from study advocated by certain Sufis. He once said to the followers of Ibn Maktum: "Busy yourself with the acquisition of some knowledge, and do not let the words of the Sufis [to the contrary] fool you. I myself used to hide my inkwell and pen inside my

---

[1]Ibn Taymiyya, *al-Risala al-Safadiyya* (1:267).

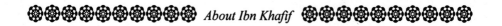

clothes, and go secretely to visit the scholars. If they [the Sufis] had found out, they would have fought me and they would have said: You will not succeed. Later they found themselves needing me."

When Ibn Khafif became too weak to stand in his habitual supererogatory prayers, he prayed double their number sitting, in view of the Prophet's 鑾 report whereby "The prayer of one sitting is half that of one standing."[2] Ibn Bakuyah related from Ibn Khafif that he said: "In my beginnings I would recite in one *rak'a* ❨*Qul huwa Allahu ahad*❩ [Sura 112] ten thousand times, or recite the entire Qur'an in one *rak'a*." "Never in forty years was the Ramadan-end purification tax *(zakât al-fitr)* incumbent upon me."[3] Al-Sulami said: "Abu 'Abd Allah came from a family of princes, but he practiced asceticism *(zuhd)* to the point that he said: 'I would collect rags from refuse-heaps, wash them, and mend whatever I could use for clothing, and I spent fourteen months breaking my fast at night with a handful of beans.'"

Al-Qushayri devoted an entire chapter to Ibn Khafif in his *al-Risala al-Qushayriyya*. Ibn al-Jawzi in *Talbis Iblis* casts aspersions on him as he usually does with the Sufis.

All the sources establish that Ibn Khafif visited al-Hallaj in prison in Baghdad upon his return from pilgrimage in the year 300. He described al-Hallaj as "a true monotheist *(muwahhid)* and knower of his Lord *('âlim rabbâni)*," although he differed with him on certain points.[4]

---

[2]Narrated from 'Imran ibn Husayn by al-Bukhari in his *Sahih*.
[3]A reference to his poverty which exempts him from the *zakât al-fitr*. See the *Reliance of the Traveller* (p. 261 h7.0) for the necessary conditions for paying it.
[4]Ibn 'Asakir, *Tabyin Kadhib al-Muftari* (p. 189-191); al-Dhahabi, *Siyar A'lam al-Nubala'* (12:413-416 #3447); al-Sulami, *Tabaqat al-Sufiyya* (p. 308); Shatta, *Sira al-Shaykh Ibn Khafif*.

Imam Ibn Khafif :
Correct Islamic Doctrine
(Al-'Aqîda al-Sahîha)[5]

I. Godhead

1.   Glory and praise to Allah Who has guided us in His paths! He has sent down the Book to us. He has lavished His gifts upon us in the persons of the Prophets. He has shown us their tracks and their means of crossing the waters. He has detailed the verses and the suras, cautioning and warning, forbidding and commanding, prohibiting, haranguing and rebuking. These verses and suras are His admonishment for those who heed admonishment, His wisdom for those who profit from wisdom. To Allah belongs all praise first and last, open and hidden! Blessings upon the best being in all creation – Muhammad, the Elect – and upon his most pure Family, the chosen ones!

2.   To proceed: Verily, the one who is endowed with reason is he who believes what is right as his preparation for meeting his Lord; who sifts clean his intentions so that he purifies his deeds; who excels in the worship of his Lord so that he supplies himself for his return; and who knows that he was not created in vain nor will he be left aimless. Therefore, let each one strive to make firm the ties of his Religion, purify his deeds, and correct his worship. There, lies Religion's completion, purity, increase, and growth. And it is Allah Who grants success in leading one to the paths of guidance and to whatever He loves and accepts.

3.   The first need of Allah's servant is belief in Absolute Oneness *(al-tawhîd)* by which all works become complete. To achieve it one must hold the following beliefs.

4.   Allah is One, but not in the sense of a sequential number *(al-'adad)* nor in that of units *(al-âhâd)*.

5.   He is "something" yet not like things *(shay'un lâ kal-ashyâ')*.[6]

[5]Published in full by Ibrahim al-Dusuqi Shatta in his *Sira Ibn Khafif* (p. 340-365). Mss. Fatih 5381, 5391, and Hagia Sophia 4792, f°s 746b-748a.

6. There is no resemblance unto Him in all His creation.

7. There is no opposite *(didd)* for Him in all His dominion.

8. There is no equal *(nidd)* for Him in all His handiwork.

9. He is neither a body *(jism)*, nor an accident *('arad)*, nor an indivisible substance *(jawhar)*.[7]

10. In no way does He subsist in originated matters[8] *(al-hawâdith)* nor they in Him.[9]

11. He does not in any way indwell anything nor does anything indwell Him.

12. He does not manifest Himself in anything *(lâ yatajallâ fi shay'in)*,[10] nor does He hide Himself *(istatara)* with anything created.

13. He is the All-Knower of what was and what shall be; of what is not to be and, if it were to be, how it would be.[11]

14. Allah was when there was nothing with Him:

15. He was [characterized as the] Knower when there was nothing to be known;[12]

16. He was [characterized as the] Powerful when there was no object of power;[13]

---

[6]Or: "He is an entity but not in the sense of created entities."

[7]"Accident" in the sense of a nonessential attribute characterizing, like "substance," created things.

[8]Or: "Contingencies."

[9]Due to the mutually exclusive nature of contingency *(hudûth)* and incontingency *(qidam)*. The former refer to whatever is created, the latter to the beginningless and uncreated, "and the twain never meet" *(lâ munasaba baynahumâ)*.

[10]Al-Tustari said: "Allah manifests Himself to creation as He wishes" *(yatajallâ lahum kayfa shâ')*. Abu Nu'aym, *Hilya al-Awliya'* (10:214 #15011).

[11]I.e. Allah knows all possibilities, whether of existent of inexistent things, and all their consequences.

[12]*[Wa ya'taqidu annahu]* *'âlimun wa lâ ma'lûm*.

17. He was [characterized as the] Seer when there was nothing to be seen;[14]

18. He was [characterized as the] Sustainer when there was nothing to be sustained;[15]

19. He was [characterized as the] Creator when there was nothing created.[16]

20. Knowledge is other than sight.[17] For He sees all existent things whereas He knows of all inexistent things, although what is non-existent is not seen nor is properly called a thing.

21. The attribute *(al-sifa)* is other than the subject of attribution *(al-mawsûf)*. It is a notion pertaining to the subject and subsisting *(qâ'im)* therein.[18]

22. Allah is knowing by [the Attribute of] knowledge and powerful by [the attribute of] power.[19]

---

[13]*Qâdirun wa lâ maqdûr.*

[14]*Râ'in wa lâ mar'iyy.*

[15]*Râziqun wa lâ marzûq.*

[16]*Khâliqun wa lâ makhlûq.*

[17]This is in refutation of Mu'tazili doctrine which negates the distinctness of the attributes of sight *(basar)* and hearing *(al-sam')* from the attribute of knowledge *('ilm)*, and dilute all three – and the other "Attributes of Forms" *(sifât al-ma'âni)* into the Essence. Al-Sanusi said: *(Hashiya al-Bajuri* p. 61-75): "Necessary for Him are seven Attributes, named *sifât al-ma'âni* ["Attributes of Forms"], which are power *(al-qudra)*, will *(al-irâda)*, knowledge *('ilm)*, life *(al-hayât)*, hearing *(al-sam')*, sight *(al-basar)*, speech *(al-kalâm)*. Next there are seven attributes called *sifât ma'nawiyya* ["Attributes Pertaining to Forms"], inseparable from the previous seven, namely: His being powerful, willing, knowing, living, hearing, seeing, and speaking." The *Mu'tazila* denied the "Attributes of Forms" but accepted the "Attributes Pertaining to Forms." Their reasoning for doing so was that Allah is perfect and complete in Himself and therefore not in need, for example, of an attribute of knowledge by which He knows, for He is All-Knowing in His essence. They claimed that the logical consequence of the "Attributes of Forms" was "multiplicity of beginningless entities" *(ta'addud al-qudamâ')*. This reasoning was refuted by the entirety of *Ahl al-Sunna* scholars. See al-Buti, *Kubra al-Yaqinat al-Kawniyya* (p. 119 n.).

[18]"The Attributes are neither the Essence Itself nor other than It *(al-sifât laysat 'aynu al-dhât wa lâ ghayraha)*, as is the school of *Ahl al-Sunna wa al-Jama'a*." Al-Qari, *Daw' al-Ma'ali* (p. 5).

[19]In refutation of the *Mu'tazila* who said "He knows with His Essence, not with an Attribute," "He is powerful in His Essence," etc. Their reasoning was that Allah is

23. The divine Attributes are obtained only from the transmitted sources, that is, either what Allah said of Himself, or what the Prophet 鐮 said of Him, or what the Muslims concur about in relation to a given attribute.

24. The divine Names are not obtained by making up surnames *(talqîban)* nor by analogical derivation *(qiyâsan)*.[20]

25. Neither the Names nor the Attributes are created.

26. Allah's Speech is from Him and goes back to Him; it is heard, written down, preserved, recited, and studied.[21]

27. He established Himself over the Throne and descends to the nearest heaven before dawn in the sense of an attribute of His, not in the sense of displacement.

28. He created Adam with His Hand – not "the Hand that is His Power" but "the Hand that is His Attribute."[22]

---

perfect and complete in Himself and therefore not in need, for example, of an attribute of knowledge by which He knows, for He is All-Knowing in His essence. They claimed that the logical consequence of the "Attributes of Forms" was "multiplicity of beginningless entities" *(ta'addud al-qudamâ')*. This reasoning was refuted by the entirety of *Ahl al-Sunna* scholars. See Buti, *Kubra al-Yaqinat al-Kawniyya* (p. 119).

[20] Or: "By using rational guidelines."

[21] Al-Sanusi (p. 70f. of *Hashiya al-Bajuri*): "The attribute of speech is without letter nor sound and relates to everything to which knowledge relates... necessary, possible, and impossible things." Scholars further defined Allah's Speech as either *kalâm nafsî* or *kalâm lafzî*. The former is what is meant in al-Sanusi's definition, while the latter refers to its recitation, which is created. See al-Buti, *Kubra al-Yaqinat* (p. 125-127).

[22] This is to preclude the negation of the attribute of Hand which the *Mu'tazila* practiced, hence al-Ash'ari's statement in the *Ibana* (Sabbagh ed. p. 101; 'Uyun ed. p. 108): "The interpretation of ❨both My Hands❩ as "My Power" [in the verse ❨that which I have created with both My hands❩ (38:75)] is false in many ways." However, the interpretation of Allah's Hands to signify power or strength is used in the Ash'ari school according to Arabic usage – as in *Lisan al-'Arab, Mukhtar al-Sihah, Mufradat Alfaz al-Qur'an,* and *al-Nihaya* – while asserting Allah's Attribute of Hand. Ibn 'Abd al-Salam said: "The meaning of the Prophet's 鐮 saying, 'The heart of the believer is between two fingers of the Merciful' [Narrated with sound chains from 'Abd Allah ibn 'Amr by Muslim and from al-Nawwas ibn Sam'an by Ahmad, al-Nasa'i, Ibn Majah, Ibn Hibban in his *Sahih*, al-Hakim, and others] is that

29. The same applies with all the sound reports that were narrated concerning the attributes. One holds them true as part of one's belief and surrenders to them without evaluation nor discussion.

30. The believers shall see Allah on the Day of Resurrection just as they see the full moon on the nights when it rises. They will not be unfairly deprived of seeing Him.[23]

31. They will see Him without encompassment *(ihâta)* nor delimitation *(tahdîd)* within any given limit *(hadd)*, whether from the front, the back, above, below, right, or left.

32. Allah is doer of what He will:

33. Injustice is not attributed to Him,

Allah exerts His custody over it with His power and determination as He wills, changing it from disbelief to belief and from obedience to disobedience or the reverse. It is like His saying: ⟨Blessed is He in Whose hand is the dominion⟩ (67:1) and: ⟨O Prophet! Say unto those captives who are in your hands⟩ (8:70). It is understood that the captives were not left in the physical hands of the Muslims but that they were subdued and conquered by them. The same applies to the expressions: "Specific and non-specific matters are in the hand of so-and-so," and "The slaves and the animals are in the hand of so-and-so." It is understood that all these mean that they are in his control *(istîlâ')* and disposal and not in his physical hand. Similarly Allah's saying: ⟨Or he agrees to forgo it in whose hand is the marriage tie⟩ (2:237). The marriage tie is not in his physical hand, but the hand is only an expression of his empowerment and his ability to dispose of the matter. For one to say: "I believe in this matter what the *Salaf* believed" is a lie. How does he believe what he has no idea about, and the meaning of which he does not know? Nor is speaking about the meaning a reprehensible innovation, but rather an obligatory excellent innovation *(bid'a hasana wâjiba)*, whenever something dubious appears. The only reason the *Salaf* kept away from such discourse is that in their time no-one construed the words of Allah and those of His Prophet to mean what it is not permissible to construe them to mean. If any such dubiousness had appeared in their time they would have shown it to be a lie and rejected it strenuously! Thus did the Companions and the Salaf refute the *Qadariyya* when the latter brought out their innovation, although they did not use to address such matters before the *Qadariyya* appeared on the scene. Nor did they reply to the individuals who mentioned them. Nor did any of the Companions relate any of it from the Prophet ﷺ since there was no need for it. And Allah knows best." Al-'Izz ibn 'Abd al-Salam, *Fatawa* (p. 55-57).

[23]See Appendix, "The Vision of Allah in the World and the Hereafter."

34. And He rules over His dominion as He will, without [anyone's entitlement to] objection whatsoever.[24]

35. His decree is not revoked nor His judgment amended.

36. He brings near Him whomever He will without [need for] cause and He removes far from Him whomever He will without [need for] cause.

---

[24]The Ash'ari position is that Allah rewards and punishes without being obliged to do so by the actions of His servants ("Allah is doer of what He will"). He is free to place the disbeliever in Paradise and the believer in Hellfire without any injustice on His part ("Injustice is not attributed to Him"), since He owns all sovereignty over the heavens and the earth, and no one received any share or authority from Him to object to what He does. This is similar to par. 36 below. The evidence for this is in the verses: **《Know you not that unto Allah belongs the Sovereignty of the heavens and the earth? He punishes whom He will, and forgives whom He will. Allah is Able to do all things.》** (5:40) **《Say : Who then can do aught against Allah, if He had willed to destroy the Messiah son of Mary, and his mother and everyone on earth? Allah's is the Sovereignty of the heavens and the earth and all that is between them. He creates what He will. And Allah is Able to do all things.》** (5:17) At the same time it is obligatorily known that Allah does not take back His promise to reward those who believe and do good and punish evil-doers: **《But as for those who believe and do good works We shall bring them into gardens underneath which rivers flow, wherein they will abide for ever. It is a promise from Allah in truth; and who can be more truthful than Allah in utterance?》** (4:122). The scholars have described the former evidence as "based on reason" *(dalil 'aqli)* and the latter as "based on law" *(dalil shar'i)*, noting that it is the latter which takes precedence over the former. Cf. al-Buti, *Kubra al-Yaqinat* (p. 149). See also below, par. 40 and note. The following debate is recorded as taking place between the Ash'ari scholar Abu Ishaq al-Isfarayini and the Mu'tazili scholar 'Abd al-Jabbar:

    'Abd al-Jabbar: "Glory to Him Who exalted Himself above indecency!"

    Abu Ishaq: "Glory to Him in Whose dominion nothing befalls but what He wills!"

    'Abd al-Jabbar: "Can our Lord will that He be disobeyed?"

    Abu Ishaq: "Can our Lord be disobeyed against His will?"

    'Abd al-Jabbar: "Do you think, if He has prevented me from being guided, that He has acted well towards me, or ill?"

    Abu Ishaq: "If he prevented you from something that you own, then He has acted ill towards you; but if He prevented you from something that He owns, then **《He selects for His mercy whom He will》** (2:105, 3:74)."

'Abd al-Jabbar remained silent. Narrated in Ibn 'Asakir's *Tabyin Kadhib al-Muftari* (p. 240-241), al-Dhahabi's *Siyar A'lam al-Nubala'* (13:225-227 #3834), and Ibn al-Subki's *Tabaqat al-Shafi'iyya al-Kubra* (4:256-262 #358).

37. His will for His servants is the exact state they are in.

38. His good pleasure is in their obedience, while their disobedience takes place by His will but without His good pleasure.

39. He gives and He withholds, He blames and He praises.

40. Acts belong to Allah, not to creatures, while earning *(al-iktisâb)* belongs to creatures, but earning is created by Allah, not by them.[25]

41. Things do not act of their own nature. Neither does water quench thirst, nor does bread sate hunger, nor does fire burn, but Allah creates satedness simultaneously with eating, and hunger at other times. Likewise, drinking is the drinker's doing while quenchedness is from Allah, and killing is the killer's doing while death is from Allah.

42. Imagination cannot perceive Him, nor knowledge encompass Him, nor reason describe Him.

43. He is the One Alone, the Unique, the Everlasting! To Him belong the most beautiful Names and most exalted Attributes. His is the Dominion here and hereafter, with glory and praise, thanksgiving, laud, and magnificence!

II. Prophethood

44. Prophethood is true. It is Allah's great proof over creation, after which they have no excuse left.

45. Our Prophet Muhammad ﷺ is the best of the Prophets and Messengers and the Seal of Prophets after whom there is no Prophet. To obey him is an absolute obligation. To contradict or contravene him is disbelief. His command is imperative except for what is established by proof to be only recommended. His [unqualified] acts constitute the Sunna.

46. The Prophet ﷺ is not like anyone of us in all respects.

---

[25]The verse which refers to *iktisab* is: ❨**Enter the Garden because of what ye used to do.**❩ (16:32). See Appendix, "The Servant's Earning of Created Deeds."

11

47. He has acquired a kind of knowledge to which creatures were not summoned.[26]

48. He knows what is and what shall be[27] and he gave news of the Unseen.

49. He was taken up bodily on the Ascension, not in vision.

50. He saw his Lord Almighty Who spoke to him, imparting to him recommendations, commands, and permissions.

51. He saw the Prophets, upon them blessings and peace.

52. He entered Paradise, and he saw Hellfire.

53. He petitioned and he was granted his request.

54. He spoke and he was heard.

55. He is the first intercessor.

56. He shall be the first to rise from the grave.

57. He shall be the first to enter Paradise.

58. Allah sent him forth to the totality of human beings and jinn.

59. The Law he brought abrogated all previous laws.

60. He has conveyed the Message fully and has exhorted the Community in truth and sincerity.

61. All his sins were forgiven, past and future.

---

[26]Or: "to which other than him cannot lay claim."
[27]"Knows" in the sense of being imparted by Allah whatever He imparted to him. Note that Ibn Khafif did not say "He knows all that is and all that shall be." (Shaykh Adib Kallas.)

62. Allah imposed upon him certain obligations which He did not impose on his Community. He has disallowed for him certain matters which He allowed for other than him.

63. All this is as marks of immense honor from Allah to the Prophet, blessings and peace upon him and upon his Family and Companions.

III. Generalities

64. Belief *(al-îmân)* is the attribute of the believer *(al-mu'min)*.

65. Declaring the absolute oneness of Allah *(tawhîd)* is the attribute of the true monotheist *(muwahhid)*.

66. Knowledge of Allah *(ma'rifa)* is the attribute of the Knower *('ârif)*.

67. Love is the attribute of the lover, all in the same way that knowledge *('ilm)* is the attribute of the possessor of knowledge *('âlim)*, and power *(qudra)* the attribute of him who possesses power.

68. Belief consists in speech, deed, and intention. It increases and decreases.

69. Belief is a light thrown into the heart, but not the light of the divine Entity.

70. Belief *(al-îmân)* is different from submission *(al-islâm)*.[28]

71. Declaring the absolute oneness of Allah *(tawhîd)* is different from knowledge of Allah *(ma'rifa)*.

72. Knowledge of Allah is different from belief.

73. Knowledge of the proofs that establish the reality of the Creator is an obligation.

---

[28]See on this notion Ibn 'Abd al-Salam's short treatise, *Ma'na al-Iman wa al-Islam* and Ibn Abi Ya'la's *Tabaqat al-Hanabila* (1:25, 2:14, 2:302).

74. Knowledge of the divine Attributes is obtained through effort, while intimate knowledge of Allah *(ma'rifa al-takhsîs)* is a divine gift.

75. The root of belief is a divine gift while the conditions of belief can be met through effort.

76. Belief, declaring the absolute oneness of Allah, and knowledge of Allah have an appearance *(zâhirun)* as well as a reality *(haqîqatun)*.

77. Every believer *(mu'min)* is a Muslim, but not every Muslim is a believer.

78. Capacity to act *(istitâ'a)* is concomitant with the act.

79. The comfort and ease of the dwellers of Paradise shall remain without end as Allah remains without end, and the punishment of the disbelievers shall remain without end as Allah remains without end.

80. The believers shall be brought out of the Fire, and great sins *(al-kabâ'ir)* will not cause those who committed them to remain therein eternally.

81. Allah does not force His servants to commit disobedience.

82. None enters Paradise by virtue of his good deeds but only by Allah's munificence, mercy, and favor.[29]

83. Paradise is real; Hellfire is real; Resurrection is real; the Rendering of Accounts is real; the Balance of Deeds is true; the Bridge [over the Fire]; the punishment of the grave is real; and the questioning of the angels Munkar and Nakîr is real.

84. The best of human beings after Allah's Messenger ﷺ is Abu Bakr, then 'Umar, then 'Uthman, then 'Ali ﷺ.

---

[29]Hadith of the Prophet ﷺ: "None is caused by his deeds to enter Paradise." They said: "Not even you, O Messenger of Allah?" He said: "No, not even I, unless Allah enfold me in favor and mercy. Therefore, endeavor to act right, act moderately, and let none of you wish for death. If he is a doer of good, perhaps his goodness shall increase; and if he is a wrong-doer, perhaps he shall relent." Narrated from Abu Hurayra and 'A'isha by al-Bukhari and from Abu Hurayra by Muslim and Ahmad.

85. The best of centuries is the one in which was sent the Prophet ﷺ, then that of the Companions, then that of the Successors.

86. After the above, the best of times and people are the best in their deeds. Those in whom we see particular merit, we bear witness to it concerning them.

87. Whoever bears the two testimonies of faith, prays in the direction of prayer, remits the purification-tax, fasts the month of Ramadan, and goes on pilgrimage to the House, we do not testify that he shall enter Paradise nor Hellfire. Nor can we testify to his unbelief except in a restricted sense.[30] It is as in Allah's saying: ❴And pilgrimage to the House is a duty unto Allah for mankind, for him who can find a way thither. As for him who disbelieves, lo! Allah is Independent of creatures.❵ (3:97) [The relevance of the verse is that] he who does not perform pilgrimage is not a disbeliever.

88. One prays behind the righteous as well as the unrighteous. One obeys the ruler even if the latter should be an Abyssinian slave.

89. Lone-narrator reports *(âhâd)* make practice obligatory but not knowledge, while mass-narrated *(mutawâtir)* reports make both knowledge and practice obligatory.[31]

90. Reason alone *(al-'aql)* cannot determine right and wrong *(lâ yuhassin wa lâ yuqabbih)*. It is the Law that holds sway over reason [in determining the licit and the unlawful].[32]

91. People are considered upright until some cause arises to the contrary.

92. All things are permissible until the proof of their prohibitiveness is established.

---

[30]Several meanings were narrated for the word *kafara* in the "verse of Pilgrimage" which the author cites, such as: Whoever disbelieves in the duty of Pilgrimage, or its reward, or the punishment of those who do not fulfill it, or in the "clear signs" mentioned in the verse, or in Allah and the Last Day, or in the House. See al-Tabari.

[31]See Appendix entitled: "Lone-narrator Reports."

[32]This is in refutation of the *Mu'tazila* who considered that reason provided a sufficient criterion for deciding right and wrong unaided by revelation.

93. The property and slaughtered meats of Muslims are licit [for transaction and consumption] except that regarding which prohibition has been narrated to us.

IV. *Tasawwuf*

We mention in the fourth section matters which address this group – the Sufis – exclusively.

94. Utter dependency *(al-faqr)* is better than sufficiency *(al-ghinâ)*.

95. Universal renunciation *(al-zuhd fî al-kulliyya)* is better than in selected matters *(fî al-ba'd)*.

96. Attainment of the Truth other than by way of worship is impossible.

97. Sight [of Allah] in the world is impossible.[33]

98. Prophethood *(nubuwwa)* is greater than sainthood *(wilâya)*, but prophethood cannot be obtained through effort.

99. "Staggering" miracles *(al-mu'jizât)* are for Prophets, while miraculous gifts *(al-karâmât)* are for saints.

100. Miraculous foresight *(al-firâsa)* can be obtained through effort, but one who is inspired *(al-muhaddath)* or spoken to [by the angels] *(al-mukallam)* is other than the one who possesses such foresight.

101. Freedom from the bond of servanthood *(al-'ubûdiyya)* is null and void, but freedom from the bond of egotism *(al-nufûsiyya)* is possible. Servanthood can never be cancelled out.[34]

---

[33]See Appendix, "The Vision of Allah in the World and the Hereafter."

[34]Servanthood is the highest attribute of human beings, as indicated in the hadith of the Prophet ﷺ whereby an angel descended as Jibril عليه السلام was sitting together with the Prophet ﷺ. Jibril said: "This angel did not descend on earth since its creation until this moment." The angel said: "O Muhammad! Your Lord told me to ask you: 'Shall I make you a king or a servant and Messenger?'" Jibril said: "Humble yourself before your Lord, O Muhammad!" The Prophet ﷺ said: "A servant and Messenger!"

102.   The attributes [of human nature] subside in those who have knowledge of Allah but they persist in the seekers *(al-murîdîn)*.

103.   Return [to normality] after attainment [of nearness to Allah] is possible.

104.   The servant is taken through various spiritual states *(ahwâl)* until he reaches a high spiritual quality. At that time he knows the Unseen, the earth is folded up for him, he can walk on water and disappear from sight.

105.   Intoxication *(al-sukr)* for the seekers is true, but for the masters it is null and void.

106.   Conditions in which Truth overwhelms *(ghalabât al-Haqq)* all things created are possible.[35]

107.   States *(al-ahwâl)* are for the intermediary levels, stations *(al-maqâmât)* are for the knowers of Allah, and strain *(al-shidda)* is for the seekers.

108.   Soberness *(sahû)* is better than intoxication.

109.   Slow progressions *(al-âmâd)* are better than sudden obliteration *(al-istilâm)*.[36]

Narrated from Abu Hurayra by Ahmad, al-Bazzar, and Abu Ya'la, the former two with a sound chain as stated by al-Haythami in *Majma' al-Zawa'id* and Ahmad Shakir in Ahmad's *Musnad* (#7160). Also see al-Mundhiri's *al-Targhib*.

[35] A reference to what Shaykh Ahmad Sirhindi called *wahda al-shuhûd*. The explanation of this state by Ibn Taymiyya in his *Majmu'a al-Fatawa* (2:396-397, 10:339) is well-known. See, for its translation, Shaykh M. Hisham Kabbani, *Islamic Beliefs and Doctrine According to Ahl al-Sunna* (p. 365-366).

[36] I.e. wayfaring *(al-sulûk)* is better than total absorption into a state of distraction *(jadhba)*, and the ordinary, sober wayfarer *(al-sâlik)* is better than the oblivious devotee *(al-majdhûb)*. The latter state enters into the "various spiritual states," the "intoxication," the "overwhelming of all created things," and the "states of the intermediary levels" mentioned in the previous five paragraphs. This is an important corrective to the false assumption that *jadhba* is preferable to ordinary *sulûk*. It was also said (by Shaykh 'Adnan Kabbani) that *al-âmâd* refers to long life and *al-istilâm* to early death. The former is better than the latter in the sense that a long life of doing good corresponds to a higher level than a brief one.

110.   The involvement of the knower in [worldly] things does not detract from his state.

111.   If reliance upon Allah *(tawakkul)* is correct, storing up provision *(al-iddikhâr)* does no harm.[37]

112.   The disobedience *('isyân)* of Prophets is a cause for their nearness to Allah and benefits for their Community. They are not called sinners *('usât)*. We say: "Adam disobeyed" *('asâ)*, but not "he is a sinner" *('âsin)*.

113.   *Tasawwuf* is neither knowledge nor deeds but an attribute with which the essence of the Sufi adorns itself, possessing knowledge and deeds, and consisting in the balance in which these two are weighed.

114.   *Tasawwuf* is different from utter dependency *(faqr)*, and Godwariness *(taqwâ)* is different from *tasawwuf*.

115.   The utterly dependent one *(al-faqîr)* is not allowed to handle material causes [of living][38] while the Sufi is.

116.   States are endless but each state ends in another state.

117.   Knowledge of Allah, belief, and affirmation of the One God are not states; nor is existence *(al-wujûd)* a state, although it accompanies the servant in his states.[39]

118.   The knowledge of those who strive to obtain knowledge of Allah *(al-mu'tarifûn)* is different from that of those upon whom knowledge of Allah is bestowed *(al-mu'arrafûn)*.[40]

---

[37]A corrective to the assumption that possessing provision jeopardizes *tawakkul*.

[38]"Your wish to handle material causes when Allah has put you in a state of dispossession *(al-tajrîd)* is a decline from a higher level." Ibn 'Ata' Allah, *Hikam* (#2).

[39]This is in keeping with al-Ash'ari's position that by "existence" is meant "what exists" or else the concept of existence. There is either existence or non-existence, and not, as some said, a "state" of existence which is a means *(wâsita)* between existence and non-existence. (Shaykh Adib Kallas.)

[40]This is a similar distinction to that between the student-seeker *(al-murîd)* and the "sought" *(al-murâd)* who achieves progress without normal effort on his part.

119.   Spiritual recital *(al-samâ')* is permissible for the knower, but null and void for the seeker.[41]

120.   Spiritual recital is neither a state nor an act of drawing near to Allah. It is better to leave it altogether because of its many evils and great dangers.

121.   All that the impassioned lover *(al-wâjid)* may find, still, he is impassioned and nothing more. Truth itself lies beyond.

122.   Whoever makes Allah the subject of erotic singing *(samma'a billâh)* commits disbelief, and whoever makes a creature the subject of singing in the lustful sense *(bî ma'na al-nufûsiyya)* commits a grave sin.

123.   However, the self-realized impassioned lover *(al-wâjid al-muhaqqiq)* is protected [from committing disbelief or grave sins].

124.   Those prone to being overcome must proceed according to whatever obligations they missed [while being overcome]. When they return to praying they make them up. Those who persist in their silence are excused.

125.   Satan does not know what is in a servant's heart and has not the least right to insinuate or whisper anything to him.[42]

126.   The self or ego *(al-nafs)* is other than the soul or spirit *(al-rûh)*, and the soul is other than the biological life *(al-hayât)*.

127.   The soul parts with the body when the latter sleeps, unlike biological life. The latter parts with the body only if the body dies. They are created.

128.   All this was readily recalled at this time. It contains a persuasive argument for you [the reader], if Allah wills. After this, keep faith in the goodness of people, their sincerity, and their loyalty. At the same time, beware of their fickleness and treachery for that is their nature.

---

[41]*Samâ'* is extensively defined in al-Qushayri's *Rasa'il* and al-Sarraj's *al-Luma'*.
[42]I.e. except with divine permission.

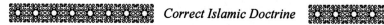 

129.   Believe firmly in the evil of your own ego, as well as in Satan's enmity and rebelliousness, so that you will save yourself from the two of them.

130.   Believe firmly in the immense favor and grace of your Protector. Keep a good opinion of Him and firm hope in the happy conclusion of your pledge in the Hereafter. For He shall not disappoint your hope nor cut short your expectation.

131.   May Allah send His blessings and peace upon the best of His creation, Muhammad, and upon his Family and Companions!

The Vision of Allah in the World and the Hereafter

Ibn Khafif stated in his *al-'Aqida al-Sahiha*:

30. The believers shall see Allah on the Day of Resurrection just as they see the full moon on the nights when it rises. They will not be unfairly deprived of seeing Him.

31. They will see Him without encompassment *(ihâta)* nor delimitation *(tahdîd)* within any given limit *(hadd)*, whether from the front, the back, above, below, right, or left. ...

97. Sight in the world is impossible.

The *Mu'tazila* and some other groups held that Allah could not be seen at all, even on the Day of Resurrection. They rejected the sound hadiths to the contrary, claiming that such vision necessitated corporeality and direction, which were precluded for Him. *Ahl al-Sunna* adduced the verse ❨**That day will faces be resplendent, Looking toward their Lord**❩ (75:22-23) and the mass-narrated hadiths to the effect that such vision will be real.

In contrast to the *Mu'tazila*, the totality of the scholars of *Ahl al-Sunna* both excluded modalities of encompassment, delimitation, direction, and other corporeal qualities and, at the same time, held that Allah will be seen by the believers in the Hereafter without specifying how. However, they differed whether such unqualified sight was possible in the world as well.

Al-Qari and al-Haytami reported that the agreement of *Ahl al-Sunna* is that sight of Allah in the world is possible but that it does not take place (except for the Prophet 鬒), while two contrary opinions on the topic are narrated from al-Ash'ari in al-Qushayri's *Risala*.[43] The proof that His sight is possible in the world was adduced by Musa's 鬒 request to Allah: ❨**My Lord! Show me Your Self, that I may gaze upon You**❩ (7:143) as Prophets

---

[43] Al-Qari, *al-Mirqat* (1892 ed. 5:303); al-Haytami, *Fatawa Hadithiyya* (p. 147-150). The latter said (p. 150): "If it is authenticated that al-Ash'ari held that the vision does take place in the world, then that position is ignored as he either did not know of the Consensus to the contrary, or took an anomalous *(shâdhdh)* stance which cannot be taken into consideration."

do not ask the impossible.[44] Imam al-Qushayri stated in the *Risala* that sight of Allah in the world does not take place for anyone except the Prophet ﷺ while al-Dhahabi, conceding that sight of Allah in the world is possible, held that it does not take place even for the Prophet ﷺ.[45] These views are based on the Prophet's ﷺ hadith: "Verily, you shall not see Allah until you die."[46] Ibn Hajar adduced the hadith: "Worship Allah as if you see Him" as further proof that there is no sight of Allah with the eyes of the head in this world but added: "The Prophet's ﷺ sight of Allah is supported by other evidence."[47]

The Prophet ﷺ saw Allah before death as is the doctrine of the majority of *Ahl al-Sunna* according to al-Nawawi and al-Qari.[48] The evidence for this is the hadith of Ibn 'Abbas whereby the Prophet ﷺ said: "I saw my Lord" *(ra'aytu rabbi)*.[49] Ibn Kathir cited it in his commentary on Sura al-Najm and declared its chain sound, but considered it part of the hadith of the dream cited below. Ibn al-Qayyim states that Imam Ahmad considered such sight to be in the Prophet's ﷺ sleep but remains a true sight – as the dreams of Prophets are true – and he adds that some of the Imam's companions mistakenly attributed to him the position that the Prophet ﷺ saw his Lord "with the eyes of his head."[50]

---

[44]As stated by al-Qari in *Sharh al-Fiqh al-Akbar*.

[45]In the *Siyar* (8:430-431).

[46]Narrated from Abu Umama ibn al-Samit al-Bahili as part of a longer hadith by Ahmad with a sound chain, as stated by al-Zayn, in the *Musnad* (16:415 #22663), Ibn Majah, al-Nasa'i in *al-Sunan al-Kubra* (4:419 #7764), al-Hakim (4:456) who stated that it is *sahih* and al-Dhahabi concurred, Ibn Abi 'Asim in *al-Ahad wa al-Mathani* (2:446 #1249) and *al-Sunna* (p. 186-187 #429) with a sound chain as stated by al-Albani, al-Ajurri in *al-Shari'a*, and Ibn Khuzayma in *al-Tawhid*. It is also narrated without mention of the Companion's name by Muslim in his *Sahih*, al-Tirmidhi who declared it *hasan sahih*, Ahmad with a sound chain (17:72 #23562), and Ibn Abi 'Asim in *al-Sunna* (p. 187 #430) with a sound chain.

[47]In *Fath al-Bari* (1959 ed. 1:125 #50).

[48]In *al-Mirqat* (5:308).

[49]Narrated by Ahmad with two chains of which one is sound, and al-Ajurri with a sound chain as stated by the editors of the former's *Musnad* (3:165 #2580, 3:184 #2634) and the latter's *al-Shari'a* (p. 495 #1047) as well as al-Haythami in *Majma' al-Zawa'id* (1:78-79). Also narrated by Ibn Abi 'Asim in *al-Sunna* (p. 188 #433) with the same chain as the second of Imam Ahmad's two narrations. Ahmad and Abu Zur'a considered this hadith authentic, as stated in *Tabaqat al-Hanabila* (1:312, 1:242), al-Suyuti's *al-La'ali'* (1:29-30), and al-Diya' al-Maqdisi's *al-Mukhtara* (1:79 #66).

[50]Ibn al-Qayyim, *Zad al-Ma'ad* (3:34).

Al-Bayhaqi also narrated the hadith "I saw my Lord" in *al-Asma' wa al-Sifat* with a sound chain but with the addition: "in the form of a curly-haired, beardless young man wearing a green robe," a condemned, disauthenticated addition and concatenation with another hadith that refers to Jibril ﷺ.[51] Hence al-Suyuti interpreted it either as a dream or, quoting his shaykh Ibn al-Humam, as "the veil of form" *(hijâb al-sûra).*[52]

The latter explanation is echoed in al-Qari's several commentaries of the similar hadith whereby the Prophet ﷺ said: "My Lord came to me in the best form – the narrator said: I think he said: 'in my sleep' – and asked me over what did the Higher Assembly *(al-mala' al-a'lâ)*[53] vie, and I said I did not know, so He put His hand between my shoulders, and I felt its coolness in my innermost, and knowledge of all things between the East and the West came to me."[54]

---

[51] Al-Bayhaqi, *al-Asma' wa al-Sifat* (al-Kawthari ed. p. 444-445; al-Hashidi ed. 2:363-364 #938). A "condemned" *(munkar)* narration according to Imam Ahmad as stated in al-Dhahabi's *Tartib al-Mawdu'at* (p. 22 #22), and according to al-Ahdab in *Zawa'id Tarikh Baghdad* (8:37-40 #1662). Al-Dhahabi also states that it is *munkar* in the *Siyar* (8:430-431), however, he seems to apply this condemnation to the entirety of the narrations in this chapter.

[52] In *al-La'ali'* (1:29-30).

[53] I.e. "the angels brought near" according to Ibn al-Athir in *al-Nihaya* and others.

[54] Narrated by al-Tirmidhi with three chains, all *sahîh* according to al-Albani: two from Ibn 'Abbas – in the first of which he said "the knowledge of all things in the heaven and the earth" while he graded the second *hasan gharîb* – and one chain from Mu'adh *(hasan sahîh)* which explicitly mentions that this took place in the Prophet's ﷺ sleep. Al-Bukhari declared the latter chain *sahîh* as stated by al-Tirmidhi in his *Sunan* and in his *'Ilal*, and it towers over all other chains, according to Ibn Hajar in *al-Isaba* (2:397), in the facts that there is no discrepancy over it among the hadith scholars and its text is undisputed (cf. al-Bayhaqi's *al-Asma' wa al-Sifat*, al-Hashidi ed. 2:78). Also narrated by Ahmad with four sound chains according to Shakir and al-Zayn: one from Ibn 'Abbas with the words "I think he said: 'in my sleep'" (3:458 #3484); one from Mu'adh which Ahmad explicitly declared *sahîh* as narrated by Ibn 'Adi in *al-Kamil* (6:2244), with the words: "I woke up and lo! I was with my Lord" (16:200 #22008); and two from unnamed Companions in which no mention is made of the Prophet's ﷺ sleep or wakefulness (13:93-94 #16574, 16:556 #23103). Al-Haythami declared the latter sound as well as other chains cited by al-Tabarani in *al-Kabir* (20:109 #216, 20:141 #290) and al-Bazzar in his *Musnad*, and he declared fair the chain narrated from Abu Umama by al-Tabarani in *al-Kabir* (8:290 #8117). See *Majma' al-Zawa'id* (7:176-179). Shaykhs 'Abd al-Qadir and Shu'ayb al-Arna'ut both declared *sahîh* the seven narrations of al-Tirmidhi and Ahmad in their edition of Ibn al-Qayyim's *Zad al-Ma'ad* (3:33-34 n. 4). Also narrated from Jabir ibn Samura by Ibn Abi 'Asim in *al-Sunna* (p. 203 #465) with a fair chain according to al-Albani.

Al-Mubarakfuri relates from Ibn Kathir and al-Haytami the position that the above vision took place in the Prophet's 🏵 sleep. This is also the position of Ibn al-Jawzi based on what he termed the best chains of this hadith.[55] Al-Haytami points out that the words "I woke up and saw my Lord" in Ahmad's narration from Mu'adh are actually changed from "I dozed off and saw my Lord" due to a copyist's corruption of "I dozed off" *(istathqaltu)* – as in al-Tirmidhi's narration from Mu'adh – into "I woke up" *(istayqaztu)*.[56]

Ahl al-Sunna scholars gave many interpretations of the above hadith. For example, al-Razi and, before him, al-Bayhaqi, interpreted the placing of Allah's Hand as His extreme consideration and attention to the Prophet 🏵, or as His immense favor to him, while its specific placing between his shoulders refers to the pouring of divine kindness and mercy into his heart, and the coolness refers to the completion and perfection of his knowledge as shown

---

Also narrated from 'Abd al-Rahman ibn 'A'ish by al-Darimi in his *Musnad* (2:170 #2149) and al-Tabarani through two chains in *al-Ahad wa al-Mathani* (5:48-50 #2585-2586) and another in *Musnad al-Shamiyyin* (1:339 #597), and from Umm al-Tufayl by al-Tabarani in *al-Ahad* (6:158 #3385). The latter chain actually states: "I saw my Lord in the best form of a beardless young man" and was rejected by al-Dhahabi in *Tahdhib al-Mawdu'at* (p. 22 #22). Also narrated from the Companion Abu Rafi' [*al-Isaba* 7:134 #9875] by al-Tabarani in *al-Kabir* (1:317 #938). Also narrated from Ibn 'Abbas by Abu Ya'la in his *Musnad* (4:475 #2608). Some fair narrations of this hadith – such as al-Tabarani's from 'Abd al-Rahman ibn 'Iyash and al-Khatib's from Abu 'Ubayda ibn al-Jarrah in *Tarikh Baghdad* (8:151) – have the words: "I saw my Lord" instead of "My Lord came to me," hence Ibn Kathir's conclusion previously cited. Al-Ahdab in *Zawa'id Tarikh Baghdad* (6:251-253) and al-Haytami also cited Abu 'Ubayda ibn al-Jarrah, Ibn 'Umar, Abu Hurayra, Anas, Thawban, and Abu Umama which brings to at least eleven (without Umm al-Tufayl) the number of Companions who narrated this hadith. The various chains and narrations of this hadith were collated and discussed by Ibn Rajab in his monograph *Ikhtiyar al-Awla fi Sharh Hadith Ikhtisam al-Mala' al-A'la*, ed. Jasim al-Dawsari (Kuwait: Dar al-Aqsa, 1406). See also: Ibn Athir, *Jami' al-Usul* (9:548-550). Among those that considered this hadith as falling below the grade of *sahih* are al-Bayhaqi in *al-Asma' wa al-Sifat* (al-Kawthari ed. p. 300, al-Hashidi ed. 2:72-79), Ibn al-Jawzi in *al-'Ilal al-Mutanahiya* (1:34), Ibn Khuzayma in *al-Tawhid* (p. 214-221) and al-Daraqutni in his *'Ilal* (6:56). Some went too far and suggested that it was forged: see al-Saqqaf, *Aqwal al-Huffaz al-Manthura li Bayan Wad' Hadith Ra'aytu Rabbi fi Ahsani Sura*, appended to his edition of Ibn al-Jawzi's *Daf' Shubah al-Tashbih*.
[55]In *Daf' Shubah al-Tashbih* (Kawthari ed. p. 32).
[56]In Al-Mubarakfuri *Tuhfa al-Ahwadhi* (9:74).

by his words "I knew all things between the East and the West."[57] Al-Qari wrote the following in the chapter on the Prophet's ﷺ turban in his book *Jam' al-Wasa'il fi Sharh al-Shama'il*, a commentary on al-Tirmidhi's *Shama'il* or "Characteristics of the Prophet":

> Whether the Prophet ﷺ saw his Lord in his sleep or whether Allah the Glorious and Exalted manifested Himself to him with a form *(bi al-tajallî al-suwarî)*, this type of manifestation is known among the masters of spiritual states and stations *(arbâb al-hâl wa al-maqâm)*, and it consists in being reminded of His qualities *(hay'atihi)* and reflecting upon His vision *(ru'yatihi)*, which is the outcome of the perfection of one's self-detachment *(takhliyatihi)* and self-adornment *(tahliyatihi)*. And Allah knows best about the states of His Prophets and Intimate Friends whom He has raised with His most excellent upbringing, and the mirrors of whose hearts He has polished with His most excellent polish, until they witnessed the Station of Divine Presence and Abiding *(maqâm al-hudûr wa al-baqâ')*, and they rid themselves of the rust of screens and extinction *(sada' al-huzûr wa al-fanâ')*. May Allah bestow on us their yearnings, may He make us taste their states and manners, and may He make us die in the condition of loving them and raise us in their group.[58]

Al-Qari goes on to quote Ibn al-Qayyim's relation from Ibn Taymiyya that when the Prophet ﷺ saw that his Lord put His hand between his shoulders, he honored that place with the extremity of the turban. Elsewhere he states:

> Ibn Sadaqa said that Abu Zur'a said: 'The hadith of Ibn 'Abbas [about the Prophet seeing His Lord] is sound *(sahîh)*, and no one denies it except a *Mu'tazili'*... Ibn al-Humam said: 'This is but the veil of form *(hijâb al-sûra)*.' It seems that he meant by this that the entire goal can be visualized if it is interpreted as a formal manifestation *(tajallî suwarî)*, as it is of necessity absurd to interpret it as a real or literal manifestation *(tajallî haqiqî)*. Allah Almighty has many forms of manifestations *(anwâ' min al-tajalliyât)* according to His Entity and Attributes. Likewise, He possesses all power and encompassing ability,

---

[57]Al-Razi, *Asas al-Taqdis*, as quoted by al-Kawthari in *Daf' Shubah al-Tashbih* (p. 32-33 n.). Cf. al-Bayhaqi, *al-Asma' wa al-Sifat* (Kawthari ed. p. 300-301).
[58]Al-Qari, *Jam' al-Wasa'il* (p. 209).

well beyond the angels and other than them, to fashion forms and appearances. Yet He is transcendent above possessing a body *(jism)*, a form *(sûra)*, and directions *(jihât)* with regard to His Entity. These considerations help solve many of the purported difficulties in the ambiguous verses and the narrations of the Attributes. Allah knows best the reality of spiritual stations and the minutiae of objectives.... If the hadith is shown to have something in its chain that indicates forgery, then fine; otherwise: the door of figurative interpretation is wide and imposes itself *(bâb al-ta'wîl wâsi'un muhattam)*.[59]

Elsewhere al-Qari states:

If this vision took place in dream, then there is no difficulty.... However, if it took place in a wakeful state *(fî al-yaqaza)*, as conveyed by the letter of Ahmad ibn Hanbal's narration [but see al-Haytami's comment quoted above], then the *Salaf* declared belief in the letter of such narrations – provided they were sound – without explaining them as one would explain the attributes of creatures. Rather, they negated modality *(al-kayfiyya)* and entrusted knowledge of their hidden meaning to Allah. For He shows to His Prophet ﷺ whatever He wishes from behind the curtains of the Unseen, including what our minds have no way of comprehending. However, to leave aside figurative interpretation *(al-ta'wîl)* in our time fosters confusion *(fitna)* in the beliefs of people, due to the dissemination of the doctrines of misguidance *(i'tiqâdât al-dalâl)*. Therefore, it is appropriate to interpret it in conformity with the Law as a possible intrepretation, not a definitive one. Accordingly, the words 'in the best form' could signify 'I saw my Lord as I was in the best form in the sense of His utmost favor and kindness to me'; or 'in the Lord's best form' in the sense that the form of something is whatever distinguishes it from something else, whether it pertains to the thing itself or to whatever part of it is being characterized. This can be applied to meanings just as it is applied to material bodies. One speaks about 'picturing a matter or a situation thus.' Allah's 'form' – and Allah knows best – would then be His specific Entity *(dhâtuhu al-makhsûsa)* separate from any other representation of the farthest levels of perfection, or the Attribute that

---

[59] Al-Qari, *al-Asrar al-Marfu'a* (2nd ed. p. 209-210 #209; 1st ed. p. 126 #478).

is specific to Him, meaning 'My Lord was more gracious and kinder than at any other time.' Thus did al-Tibi and al-Tawrabashti relate it.[60]

The above is reminiscent of Ibn al-Jawzi's similar interpretation in the second hadith of his *Daf' Shubah al-Tashbih*:

If we say that he ﷺ saw Him while awake, then the form, if we say that it refers to Allah Almighty, would mean: "I saw Him in the best of His Attributes in turning to me and being pleased with me." If we say that it refers to the Prophet ﷺ himself, then it would mean: "I saw Him as I was in the best form."[61]

Others considered Ibn 'Abbas' narration to refer to a vision with the eyes of the heart, as elucidated by Ibn 'Abbas' other narrations in *Sahih Muslim* and al-Tirmidhi *(hasan)*: "He saw him with his heart." Another narration from Ibn 'Abbas in Muslim states: "He saw him with his heart twice," in commentary of the verses: ❴**The heart lied not (in seeing) what it saw**❵ (53:11), ❴**And verily he saw him, yet another time**❵ (53:13).

Another explanation is that the Prophet ﷺ saw light. This is stated explicitly in the Prophet's ﷺ reply, when asked by Abu Dharr if he had actually seen his Lord: "I saw light."[62]

Many sound reports show that the Companions differed sharply whether the Prophet ﷺ saw Allah or not. Ibn 'Abbas related that he did, while Ibn Mas'ud, 'A'isha, Abu Hurayra, and Abu Dharr related reports to the contrary, stating that the verses of Sura al-Najm and other Suras referred to Jibril, and that the Prophet ﷺ said that he saw light.

Al-Bukhari narrated from Masruq that the latter said:

I said to 'A'isha: "O my mother! Did Muhammad ﷺ see his Lord?" She replied: "My hair stands on end because of what you said.

---

[60]Al-Mubarakfuri in *Tuhfa al-Ahwadhi* (9:73-74) quotes the above comments from al-Qari's *al-Mirqat* only to reject them on the grounds that they contravene – in his view – the method of the *Salaf*, a proof of his leaning towards unenlightened literalism.

[61]Ibn al-Jawzi, *Daf' Shubah al-Tashbih* (Kawthari ed. p. 32).

[62]Narrated by Muslim, al-Tirmidhi *(hasan)*, and Ahmad through four chains.

Have you no idea of three things – whoever tells them to you is lying? [First,] whoever tells you that Muhammad ﷺ saw his Lord, is lying." She then recited: 〈Vision comprehends Him not, but He comprehends (all) vision. He is the Subtle, the Aware.〉 (6:103) 〈And it was not (vouchsafed) to any mortal that Allah should speak to him unless (it be) by revelation or from behind a veil〉 (42:51). "[Second,] whoever tells you that he knows what shall happen tomorrow, is lying." She then recited: 〈No soul knoweth what it will earn tomorrow〉 (31:34). "And [third,] whoever tells you that he concealed something, is lying." She then recited: 〈O Messenger! Make known that which has been revealed unto you from your Lord, for if you do it not, you will not have conveyed His message. Allah will protect you from mankind. Lo! Allah guides not the disbelieving folk.〉 (5:67) "However, he did see Jibril عليه السلام in his actual form twice."

This hadith is also narrated from Masruq by Muslim thus:

I was sitting back in 'A'isha's house when she said: "O Abu 'A'isha [i.e. Masruq], there are three things, whoever says any of which, he is lying about Allah in the most hateful manner." I asked: "Which things?" She said: "[First,] whoever tells you that Muhammad ﷺ saw his Lord, he is lying about Allah in the most hateful manner." I was sitting back, so I sat up and said: "O Mother of the Believers! Give me a moment and do not rush me. Did not Allah Almighty say: 〈Surely he beheld him on the clear horizon〉 (81:23), 〈And verily he saw him, yet another time〉 (53:13)?" She replied: "I am the first in this entire Community to have asked Allah's Messenger ﷺ about this, and he said: 'It is but Jibril, I did not see him in the actual form in which he was created other than these two times. I saw him alighting from the heaven, covering it all. The magnitude of his frame spans what lies between the heaven and the earth.'" Then she said: "Did you not hear Allah say: 〈Vision comprehends Him not, but He comprehends (all) vision. He is the Subtle, the Aware〉 (6:103)? Did you not hear Allah say: 〈And it was not (vouchsafed) to any mortal that Allah should speak to him unless (it be) by revelation or from behind a veil, or (that) He sends a messenger to reveal what He will by His leave. Lo! He is Exalted, Wise〉 (42:51)?" She continued: "[Second,] whoever claims that Allah's Messenger ﷺ concealed any part of Allah's Book, he is lying about Allah in the most hateful manner when Allah is saying: ❮**O Messenger! Make known that which has been revealed unto you from your Lord, for if you do it not, you will not have conveyed His message**❯ (5:67)." She continued: "[Third,] whoever claims that he can tell what shall happen tomorrow, he is lying about Allah in the most hateful manner, since Allah is saying: ❮**Say: None in the heavens and the earth knoweth the Unseen save Allah [and they know not when they will be raised again]**❯ (27:65)."[63]

Muslim mentions another wording which adds the phrase:

She said: "If Muhammad ﷺ had concealed anything of what was revealed to him, he would have concealed this verse: ❮**And when you said unto him on whom Allah has conferred favor and you have conferred favor: Keep your wife to yourself, and fear Allah. And you did hide in your mind that which Allah was to bring to light, and you did fear mankind whereas Allah had a better right that you should fear Him**❯ (33:37)."

A narration by al-Tirmidhi from al-Sha'bi cites the two positions in context:

Ibn 'Abbas met Ka'b [al-Ahbar] in 'Arafa and asked him about something, whereupon Ka'b began to shout *Allahu Akbar!* until the mountains answered him. Ibn 'Abbas said: "We are the Banu Hashim!"[64] Ka'b said: "Allah has apportioned His vision and His speech between Muhammad and Musa. Musa spoke with Him twice and Muhammad saw him twice." Masruq said: "Later[65] I went to visit 'A'isha and asked: 'Did Muhammad see his Lord?' She replied: 'You have said something that makes my hair stand on end.' I said: 'Do not

---

[63] Also narrated from Masruq by al-Tirmidhi *(hasan sahih)*.

[64] Al-Tibi said: "[Ibn 'Abbas said] this in order to urge him to be quiet, stop his irritation, and reflect upon the answer, meaning: 'We are people of science and knowledge, we do not ask about things which should be considered so far-fetched.' Because of this, he reflected and gave him his answer." In al-Mubarakfuri, *Tuhfa al-Ahwadhi* (9:118 #3496).

[65] Al-Tibi said: "It appears from this wording that Masruq was present at the time of the exchange that took place between Ka'b and Ibn 'Abbas." In al-Mubarakfuri, *Tuhfa al-Ahwadhi* (9: 119).

.rush!' and recited [the verses which conclude with][66] the verse ❨Verily he saw one of the greater revelations of his Lord❩ (53:18). She said: 'Where is this taking you? It was but Jibril. Whoever tells you that Muhammad saw his Lord, or concealed something which he was commanded [to reveal], or knew the five things which Allah mentioned ❨Lo! Allah! With Him is knowledge of the Hour. He sends down the rain [and knows that which is in the wombs. No soul knows what it will earn tomorrow, and no soul knows in what land it will die. Lo! Allah is Knower, Aware]❩ (31:34) – he has told an enormous lie. Rather, he saw Jibril, whom he did not see in his actual form except twice: once at the Lote-Tree of the Farthest Boundary *(sidra al-muntaha)*, and once in Jiyâd [in Mecca], with his six hundred wings, he had filled the firmament."

Ibn Hajar analyzed this issue at length in his works[67] and compiled a monograph on the topic titled *al-Ghunya fi al-Ru'ya*. Al-Qari also gave an authoritative discussion of the topic in *al-Mirqat*.[68]

---

[66]This gloss is by al-Tibi, who said: "It is confirmed by al-Tirmidhi's other narration stating: 'O Mother of the Believers! Give me a moment and do not rush me. Did not Allah Almighty say: ❨And verily he saw him, yet another time❩ (53:13), ❨Surely he beheld him on the clear horizon❩ (81:23)?'" Al-Mubarakfuri confirmed al-Tibi's reading. In *Tuhfa al-Ahwadhi* (9: 119).
[67]Cf. *Fath al-Bari* (1959 ed. 1:125-135 #50, 8:608-610, 11:463-469 #6204) and *al-Isaba* (2:405-406).
[68]*Al-Mirqat* (5:306f.).

The Servant's Earning of Deeds Created by Allah
(Dr. M.S.R. al-Buti)[69]

A question which might arise in the minds of some people is: "If everything is according to *qadâ'* and *qadar*, then the believer is foreordained by Allah to be a believer, and the disbeliever is foreordained by Allah to be a disbeliever. Therefore, the disbeliever's disbelief is not by his free choice, nor is the believer's belief by his free choice." ... I direct you to what I said in great detail and at length in my book *Al-Insanu Musayyarun aw Mukhayyar?* ("Is Man Controlled or Endowed With Free Choice?"). I believe that I answered this problem there in great detail. However, I shall answer now succinctly.

Everything is by *qadâ'* and *qadar*, just as Allah's Messenger ﷺ says, including helplessness and intelligence.[70] Allah's foreordained destinies are two kinds. The first kind is directly created by Allah Almighty. This is all part of "the world of creation" *('âlam al-khalq)*: stars and their orbits, the order of the universe which is unrelated to man's free choice, human birth and death, human illness and cure, vegetation, earthquakes, eclipses – all these matters are part of Allah's foreordainment and created by Him directly, without any part for free choice. This comes under the heading of "creation" in the verse ❬His verily is all creation and commandment❭ (7:54). The Creator does not make you in any way responsible for what He created without any choice on your part. ❬Allah tasks not a soul beyond its scope❭ (2:286).

The second kind of foreordained destinies is what Allah has foreordained – and what is foreordainment? It is Allah's knowledge of what shall take place. Allah only creates something in correspondence with *(tilqâ')* His knowledge. This second kind of foreordained destinies is one that takes effect or circulates through the free choices of human beings. For example: your prayer, your fasting, your pilgrimage, your purification-tax *(zakât)*, your acts of obedience, your acts of piety, your acts of disobedience – we seek refuge in Allah! – and all your deeds freely undertaken: are they foreordained

---

[69]From his unpublished commentary on Ibn 'Ata' Allah's *Hikam*.

[70] "Everything is by *qadar*, including helplessness and intelligence." Narrated from Anas and Ibn 'Umar by Muslim; from Ibn 'Umar by Ahmad and Malik; and from Ibn 'Abbas by Bukhari in his *Tarikh*. The latter narrates it both with *qada'* and *qadar*.

by Allah or not? They are foreordained by Allah, in the sense that Allah knows that you will pray by choice. When, according to Allah's knowledge, you rose to pray, He put you in a position to pray *(aqdaraka 'ala salâtik)* and created in your entity the motions of your prayer. He is the Creator [of all this]. Allah knows that you will perform pilgrimage to the Sacred House. At the time you determined to go on pilgrimage, He put you in a position to do so and created for you the causes that facilitate it for you. Allah knows that So-and-so will disobey Him by drinking wine. At the time he finally determined to drink wine, Allah put him in a position to do so and created in his hand, his feet, and his mouth the power to do it.

So then Who is the Creator of the acts of obedience? Allah. And Who is the Creator of the acts of disobedience? Allah. But to what does reward and punishment apply? Reward and punishment do not apply to the actual deed which is created by Allah, but to the resolution *(al-qasd)*, the "earning" *(al-kasb)* as Allah Almighty said: *lahâ ma kasabat wa 'alayhâ ma iktasabat* – ❨**For it is what it has earned, and against it is what it has deserved**❩ (2:286). If I determine to come to this place so that we should remind each other of one of the matters of this Religion, and say: "*Yâ Allâh!* O my Lord, I have determined to do this"– at that time the Creator creates power in my person, enables me to walk and come here, and when I sit in this place He enables me to think. He does all this, but on the Day of Resurrection what will He reward me for? Will He reward me for something which He Himself created? Rather, He will only reward me for my having determined *(qasadtu)*. And so Allah has made my act subservient to my determination.

Lone-Narrator Reports

The lone-narrator report *(khabar al-wâhid)* lexically means something narrated by only one person, and in hadith nomenclature, any report that does not reach the conditions of mass narration *(tawâtur)*, whether narrated by one, two, or more narrators.[71] *Ahl al-Sunna* concur, unlike the *Mu'tazila*, that the lone-narrator reports that are authenticated – "acceptable" *(maqbûl)* in hadith nomenclature – are obligatory to believe and put into practice. Al-Qari relates, on this point, the consensus of the Companions and the Successors.[72] Where scholars differ is whether the same hadiths convey certainty of knowledge *(al-'ilm al-yaqînî)* or only the compelling assumption of truth *(al-zann al-ghâlib)*. These two categories differ insofar as obligatory practice and belief based on certainty of knowledge cannot be denied except on pains of apostasy, while the denial of obligatory practice and belief based on reports compellingly assumed to be true do not constitute apostasy but constitute sin. Thus if one disbelieves in a sound lone-narrator report one commits a grave transgression *(fisq)* and is even considered misguided *(dâll)*, but does not leave the fold of Islam.[73] This is unlike disbelief in a mass-transmitted report or in a verse of the Qur'an.

Ibn Khafif said in *Al-'Aqida al-Sahiha*:

> 89. Lone-narrator reports *(âhâd)* make practice obligatory, but not knowledge *(yûjib al-'amal lâ al-'ilm)*, while mass-narrated *(mutawâ-tir)* reports make both knowledge and practice obligatory.

The meaning of the above position is that it is obligatory to integrate the content of an accepted lone-narrator report into one's Islamic practice and belief; however, such a report does not impose the certainty of knowledge of a mass-transmitted report.

The scholars classified the truth of acceptable reports into "definitive" *(qat'î)* and "assumed" *(zannî)*. All of them agree that a mass-narrated report is *qat'î al-thubût* – "definitely established," while a non-mass-narrated

---

[71] Al-Qari, *Sharh Sharh Nukhba al-Fikar* (p. 209).
[72] *Ibid.* (p. 211).
[73] Al-Shafi'i, *al-Risala* (p. 460-461): "If one disbelieves in them [*âhâd* reports], we do not say to him: 'Repent!'"

accepted hadith is *zannî al-thubût* – "assumed to be established." However, the latter assumption carries various degrees of strength, the highest of which, according to Ibn Hajar and others, reaches definiteness. For example, if a lone-narrated hadith is narrated in the two *Sahih*s, has several (non-discrepant) chains of transmission, and counts among its narrators great imams such as Malik and al-Shafi'i, "then it would not be far-fetched to declare it definitely true, and Allah knows best."[74] At the same time Ibn Hajar warned: "All the types of non-*mutawâtir* hadith which we have mentioned do not result in [certainty of] knowledge regarding their veracity except to the scholar of hadith who has reached the level of expertise, knows the situations of the narrators, and is fully acquainted with the minute defects of hadith."[75]

Thus certain "attendant features" *(qarâ'in)* raise the accepted lone-narrated hadith closer or up to the level of definitive, obligatory knowledge as already illustrated by Ibn Hajar's words, and as stated by the scholars of *usûl*.[76] Among them are those mentioned by Ibn Hajar – the acceptance of the report by the entire Community, lack of discrepancy among its various narrations, and soundness of their chains of transmission. Examples of such hadiths are those that concern the punishment of the grave.[77]

All of the scholars further agree, as already stated, that a non-mass-narrated accepted hadith, although merely *zannî al-thubût*, possesses the following properties:

- Belief in it is obligatory *(al-tasdîq bihi wâjib)*
- Denying it is a grave transgression *(inkâruhu fisq)*

Beyond the above, the scholars disagreed on the point brought up by Ibn Khafif. Some have held that we are obliged only to assume as true accepted lone-narrator reports, although they do make belief and practice

---

[74]Ibn Hajar, *Sharh Nukhba al-Fikar* (p. 232).
[75]Ibn Hajar, *Sharh Nukhba al-Fikar* (p. 230-231). The knowledge of the expert is named by by Dr. 'Itr al-'ilm al-nazarî al-yaqînî ghayr al-darûrî and he places it midway between al-'ilm al-yaqînî al-qat'î al-darûrî which is absolutely binding, and 'ilm ghalaba al-zann, which is relatively binding. From the inaugural lecture to the Preparatory Class of Abu al-Nur Institute, Damascus, October 1997.
[76]Cf. al-Ghazali, *al-Mustasfa* (1:135-136); al-Amidi, *al-Ihkam fi Usul al-Ahkam*, Part 1, section entitled *Fi Haqiqa al-Khabar al-Wahid*.
[77]Cf. al-Sarakhsi, *al-Usul* (1:329-330 *Bab fi Qabul Akhbar al-Ahad*); al-Pazdawi, *al-Usul* (1:696).

obligatory since such assumption is compelling *(yufid al-zann al-ghâlib)* and thus precludes doubt. This is the position of Ibn Khafif and the Ash'aris, in conformity with the vast majority *(al-jumhûr)* of *Ahl al-Sunna* as stated by Ibn 'Abd al-Barr:

> What the majority of the people of knowledge believe is as follows: Some hold that the lone-narrated hadith make practice obligatory but not knowledge *(yûjib al-'amal dûna al-'ilm)*. This is the position of al-Shafi'i and the vast majority of the jurists and the scholars of principles. To them, the lone-narrated hadith does not make knowledge obligatory except on oath, providing definite preclusion of falsehood, and if there is no disagreement concerning it.[78]

An illustration for the acceptance of lone-narrated hadiths on provision of oath is given by 'Ali ibn Abi Talib ﷺ: "When I heard something from Allah's Messenger, Allah would benefit me with it as He wished; but when Someone other than him narrated it to me, I would make him swear to it; if he took an oath, I would believe him."[79] Ibn 'Abd al-Barr goes on to say that part of the scholars of hadith and some of the scholars of principles consider that lone-narrated hadiths make both external knowledge[80] and practice obligatory. He concludes: "Our position is that they make practice obligatory but not knowledge... and that is the position of most jurists and hadith scholars."[81] It is also the position of al-Bukhari and Ahmad[82] as well as later scholars.[83] Their position on doctrinal matters conveyed by *âhâd* reports is given by al-Bayhaqi:

---

[78]Ibn 'Abd al-Barr, *al-Tamhid* (1:7).

[79]Narrated by al-Tirmidhi *(hasan)*, Abu Dawud with a sound chain, Ahmad with two chains in the *Musnad* and also in *Fada'il al-Sahaba* (1:159 #142), and Abu Ya'la and al-Humaydi in their *Musnad*s. It is cited in the books of *Tafsir* for the verse: ❴Yet **whoso does evil or wrongs his own soul, then seeks pardon of Allah, will find Allah Forgiving, Merciful.** ❵ (4:110)

[80]By external knowledge is meant knowledge of obligations and prohibitions as opposed to internal knowledge which concerns doctrine.

[81]Ibn 'Abd al-Barr, *al-Tamhid* (1:7).

[82]Cf. al-Saqqaf, *Sahih Sharh al-'Aqida al-Tahawiyya* (p. 141-142).

[83]Cf. al-Ghazali in *al-Mustasfa*, Ibn al-Salah in *'Ulum al-Hadith*, al-'Iraqi in *Sharh 'Ulum al-Hadith*, Ibn Kathir in *Mukhtasar 'Ulum al-Hadith*, al-Nawawi in *Sharh Muqaddima Muslim*, al-Qasimi in *Qawa'id al-Tahdith*, and the contemporary authorities such as Abu Zahra, Muhammad al-Khudari, al-Ghazzali, and al-Qaradawi, all as quoted from Samer Islambuli's *al-Ahad, al-Naskh, al-Ijma'* (p. 27-30). Also see

The perspicuous scholars *(ahl al-nazar)* among our [Shafi'i] companions relinquish the use of lone-narrated reports as proofs in the divine
Attributes if such reports do not have a foundation in the Qur'an or in
scholarly consensus. Instead, they interpret them figuratively.[84]

Others dissented, such as Ibn al-Qayyim and, lately, al-Albani,
claiming that not only are *âhâd*-based belief and practice obligatory, but we
are also obliged to know them as definitely true *(yufīd al-'ilm al-qat'ī)* and
they consider them part of obligatory doctrinal knowledge.[85] These
classifications can be summarized in the following table:[86]

Ahad Sound Report on 'aqîda	Those who say: "It imparts knowledge"	Those who say: "It does not impart it"
Its transmission chain?	Assumed veracity	Assumed veracity
Belief in it?	Obligatory	Obligatory
Its rejection?	Grave transgression	Grave transgression
What does it impart?	Definitive knowledge (al-Albani)	Compelling assumption *(al-jumhûr)*

The position that sound *âhâd* impart definitive knowledge is a weak
position since it blurs the unanimous, vital distinction between *mutawâtir* and
Qur'anic reports on the one hand, and all other reports. An additional
inconsistency of that position is its contradictory labeling of lone-narrated
reports as "assumed" in the veracity of their transmission chains and yet
"definitive" in the knowledge they impart. Some have reacted to these errors
with another weak stand which consists in dismissing any and all lone-
narrator reports as something one is free to reject, especially in the chapter of
doctrine. Hence Dr. Nur al-Din 'Itr characterized these contemporary
positions with regard to *âhâd* hadiths as straddling two extremes: "Some
exaggerate in accepting the sound lone-narrated hadith to the point that they
seem to think none but they put it into practice, while others exaggerate to the

---

al-Khatib in *al-Kifaya fi 'Ilm al-Riwaya* (p. 34-48) and 'Abd al-Qahir al-Baghdadi in
Usul al-Din (p. 12).
[84]Al-Bayhaqi, *al-Asma' wa al-Sifat* (al-Kawthari ed. p. 357, al-Hashidi ed. 2:201).
[85]Cf. Ibn al-Qayyim, al-Albani in his essay entitled "The Lone-Narrated Hadith is a
Proof in Itself," and those who followed them.
[86]Adapted from Islambuli's *al-Ahad* (p. 41).

point that they seem to consider the lone-narrated hadith as nothing binding."[87]

Finally, the Consensus of the scholarly Community of *Ahl al-Sunna* take precedence over the lone-narrated hadith in the hierarchy of juridical sources in the Religion. Al-Shafi'i said: "Consensus is greater than an lone-narrated hadith."[88] Al-Khatib explained: "This means that when a consensus is opposed by a lone-narrated hadith, the latter cannot be cited as proof.[89]

---

[87]From the inaugural lecture to the Preparatory Class of Abu al-Nur Institute, Damascus, October 1997.
[88]*Siyar A'lam an-Nubala'* (10/20), *Hilya* (9:105), Ibn Abi Hatim's *Adab al-Shafi'i* (p. 231) and others.
[89]Al-Khatib al-Baghdadi, *Al-Faqih wa al-Mutafaqqih* (1:132).

BIBLIOGRAPHY

'Abd al-Qahir al-Baghdadi. *Usul al-Din*. Istanbul: Dar al-Funun fi Madrasa al-Ilahiyyat, 1928.

Abu Nu'aym al-Asfahani. *Hilya al-Awliya' wa Tabaqat al-Asfiya'*. 12 vols. Ed. Mustafa 'Abd al-Qadir 'Ata. Beirut: Dar al-Kutub al-'Ilmiyya, 1997.

Abu Ya'la al-Musili. *Musnad*. 13 vols. Ed. Husayn Salim Asad. Damascus: Dar al-Ma'mun li al-Turath, 1984.

Al-Ahdab, Khaldun. *Zawa'id Tarikh Baghdad 'Ala al-Kutub al-Sitta*. 10 vols. Damascus: Dar al-Qalam, 1996.

Ahmad ibn Hanbal. *Fada'il al-Sahaba*. 2 vols. Ed. Wasi Allah Muhammad 'Abbas. Beirut: Mu'assasa al-Risala, 1983.

-------. *Al-Musnad*. 20 vols. Ed. Ahmad Shakir and Hamza Ahmad al-Zayn. Cairo: Dar al-Hadith, 1995.

Al-Ajurri. *Al-Shari'a*. Ed. 'Abd al-Razzaq al-Mahdi. Beirut: Dar al-Kitab al-'Arabi, 1996.

Al-Ash'ari, Abu al-Hasan. *Al-Ibana 'an Usul al-Diyana*. Ed. Fawqiyya H. Mahmud. Cairo: Dar al-Ansar, 1977.

-------. *Al-Ibana 'an Usul al-Diyana*. Ed. 'Abbas Sabbagh. Beirut: Dar al-Nafa'is, 1994.

-------. *Al-Ibana 'an Usul al-Diyana*. Ed. Bashir Muhammad 'Uyun. Damascus and Beirut: Dar al-Bayan, 1996.

Al-Bajuri. *Hashiya 'ala Matn al-Sanusiyya fi al-'Aqida*. Ed. 'Abd al-Salam Shannar. Damascus: Dar al-Bayruti, 1994.

Al-Bayhaqi, Abu Bakr. *Al-Asma' wa al-Sifat*. Ed. Muhammad Zahid al-Kawthari. Beirut: Dar Ihya' al-Turath al-'Arabi, n.d. Reprint of the 1358H. Cairo edition.

-------. *Al-Asma' wa al-Sifat*. 2 vols. Ed. 'Abd Allah al-Hashidi. Riyad: Maktaba al-Sawadi, 1993.

Al-Buti. *Kubra al-Yaqinat al-Kawniyya*. Beirut and Damascus: Dar al-Fikr, 1997.

Al-Daraqutni. *Al-'Ilal*. 9 vols. Ed. Mahfuz al-Rahman Zayn Allah al-Salafi. Riyadh: Dar Tiba, 1985.

Al-Darimi. *Musnad*. 2 vols. Ed. Fu'ad Ahmad Zamarli and Khalid al-Sab' al-'Ilmi. Beirut: Dar al-Kitab al-'Arabi, 1987.

Al-Dhahabi. *Siyar A'lam al-Nubala'*. 19 vols. Ed. Muhibb al-Din al-'Amrawi. Beirut: Dar al-Fikr, 1996.

-------. *Tartib al-Mawdu'at li Ibn al-Jawzi*. Ed. Kamal ibn Basyuni Zaghlul. Beirut: Dar al-Kutub al-'Ilmiyya, 1994.

Al-Hakim. *Al-Mustadrak 'Ala al-Sahihayn*. With al-Dhahabi's *Talkhis al-Mustadrak*. 5 vols. Indexes by Yusuf 'Abd al-Rahman al-Mar'ashli. Beirut: Dar al-Ma'rifa, 1986.

Al-Haythami, Nur al-Din. *Majma' al-Zawa'id wa Manba' al-Fawa'id*. 3rd ed. 10 vols. Beirut: Dar al-Kitab al-'Arabi, 1982.

Ibn 'Abd al-Salam. *Fatawa*. Ed. 'Abd al-Rahman ibn 'Abd al-Fattah. Beirut: Dar al-Ma'rifa, 1986.

-------. *Ma'na al-Iman wa al-Islam aw al-Farq Bayn al-Iman wa al-Islam.* Ed. Iyad Khalid al-Tabba'. Beirut and Damascus: Dar al-Fikr, 1995[2].

Ibn Abi 'Asim. *Al-Ahad wa al-Mathani.* 6 vols. Ed. Basim Faysal al-Jawabira. Riyadh: Dar al-Raya, 1991.

-------. *Al-Sunna.* Ed. M. Nasir al-Din al-Albani. Beirut and Damascus: Al-Maktab al-Islami, 1993.

Ibn Abi Ya'la. *Tabaqat al-Hanabila.* 2 vols. Ed. Muhammad Hamid al-Fiqqi. Cairo: Dar Ihya' al-Kutub al-'Arabiyya, n.d.

Ibn 'Adi. *Al-Kamil fi Du'afa' al-Rijal.* 7 vols. Ed. Yahya Mukhtar Ghazawi. Beirut: Dar al-Fikr, 1988.

Ibn 'Asakir. *Tabyin Kadhib al-Muftari Fi Ma Nasaba ila al-Imam Abi al-Hasan al-Ash'ari.* Ed. Ahmad Hijazi al-Saqqa. Beirut: Dar al-Jil, 1995.

Ibn 'Ata' Allah. *Al-Hikam.* Ed. and trans. Paul Nwiya. In *Ibn 'Ata' Allah et la naissance de la confrerie shadhilite.* Beirut: Dar al-Machreq, 1990.[2]

Ibn al-Athir. *Al-Nihaya fi Gharib al-Athar.* 5 vols. Eds. Tahir Ahmad al-Zawi and Mahmud Muhammad al-Tabbakhi. Beirut: Dar al-Fikr, 1979.

Ibn Hajar. *Fath al-Bari Sharh Sahih al-Bukhari.* 14 vols. Notes by 'Abd al-'Aziz ibn Baz. Beirut: Dar al-Kutub al-'Ilmiyya, 1989. Includes al-Bukhari's *Sahih.*

-------. *Ibidem.* 13 vols. Ed. Muhammad Fouad 'Abd al-Baqi and Muhibb al-Din al-Khatib. Beirut: Dar al-Ma'rifa, 1959.

-------. *Ibidem.* Cairo: al-Matba'a al-Bahiyya, 1348 H.

-------. *Al-Isaba fi Tamyiz al-Sahaba.* 8 vols. Calcutta, 1853.

-------. *Sharh Nukhba al-Fikar.* With 'Ali al-Qari's commentary, *Sharh Sharh Nukhba al-Fikar.* Ed. Muhammad and Haytham Nizar Tamim. Beirut: Dar al-Arqam, n.d.

Ibn al-Jawzi. *Daf' Shubah al-Tashbih bi Akuff al-Tanzih.* Ed. Hasan 'Ali al-Saqqaf. Amman: Dar al-Imam Nawawi, 1991.

-------. *Daf' Shubah al-Tashbih bi Akuff al-Tanzih.* Ed. Muhammad Zahid al-Kawthari. Reprint Cairo: al-Maktaba al-Azhariyya li al-Turath, 1998.

-------. *Al-'Ilal al-Mutanahiya fi al-Ahadith al-Wahiya.* 2 vols. Ed. Shaykh Khalil al-Mays. Beirut: Dar al-Kutub al-'Ilmiyya, 1983.

Ibn Khuzayma. *Kitab al-Tawhid.* Ed. Muhammad Khalil Harras. Beirut: Dar al-Kutub al-'Ilmiyya, 1992. Reprint of Cairo 1388H. edition.

Ibn Majah. *Sunan.* See al-Suyuti *et al., Sharh Sunan Ibn Majah.*

Ibn Qayyim al-Jawziyya. *Zad al-Ma'ad fi Hadi Khayr al-'Ibad.* 6 vols. Eds. 'Abd al-Qadir al-Arna'ut and Shu'ayb al-Arna'ut. Beirut: Mu'assasa al-Risala, 1997.

Ibn al-Subki. *Tabaqat al-Shafi'iyya al-Kubra.* 10 vols. Ed. Mahmud M. al-Tannahi and 'Abd al-Fattah M. al-Hilw. 2nd. ed. Jiza: Dar Hijr, 1992.

Ibn Taymiyya. *Majmu' Fatawa Ibn Taymiyya.* 36 vols. Cairo, 1984.

-------. *Al-Risala al-Safadiyya.* Riyad: Matabi' Hanifa, 1976.

Islambuli, Samer. *Al-Ahad, al-Naskh, al-Ijma'.* Damascus: al-Hikma, 1995.

Kabbani, Shaykh Muhammad Hisham. *Islamic Beliefs and Doctrine According to Ahl al-Sunna.* Vol. 1. MountainView: Al-Sunna Foundation of America, 1996.

Al-Khatib al-Baghdadi. *Al-Faqih wa al-Mutafaqqih.* Ed. Isma'il al-Ansari. Beirut: Dar al-Kutub al-'Ilmiyya, 1980.

-------. *Al-Kifaya fi 'Ilm al-Riwaya.* 2nd ed. Ed. Ahmad 'Umar Hashim. Beirut: Dar al-Kitab al-'Arabi, 1986.

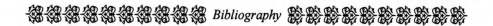

-------. *Tarikh Baghdad*. 14 vols. Madina: al-Maktaba al-Salafiyya, n.d. See also al-Ahdab, *Zawa'id Tarikh Baghdad*.

Al-Mubarakfuri. *Tuhfa al-Ahwadhi bi Sharh Jami' al-Tirmidhi*. 10 vols. Beirut: Dar al-Kutub al-'Ilmiyya, 1990. Includes al-Tirmidhi's *Sunan*.

Muslim. *Sahih*. See al-Nawawi, *Sharh Sahih Muslim*.

Al-Nasa'i. *Sunan*. See al-Suyuti, *Sharh Sunan al-Nasa'i*.

-------. *Al-Sunan al-Kubra*. 6 vols. Eds. 'Abd al-Ghaffar Sulayman al-Bandari and Sayyid Kisrawi Hasan. Beirut: Dar al-Kutub al-'Ilmiyya, 1991.

Al-Nawawi. *Sharh Sahih Muslim*. 18 vols. Ed. Khalil al-Mays. Beirut: Dar al-Kutub al-'Ilmiyya, n.d. Includes Muslim's *Sahih*.

Al-Qari. *Al-Asrar al-Marfu'a fi al-Ahadith al-Mawdu'a. (Al-Mawdu'at al-Kubra)*. 2nd ed. Ed. Muhammad ibn Lutfi al-Sabbagh. Beirut and Damascus: al-Maktab al-Islami, 1986. [1st ed. 1971.]

-------. *Daw' al-Ma'ali Sharh Bad' al-Amali*. A commentary on 'Ali ibn 'Uthman al-Awshi's poem *Bad' al-Amali*. Bulaq: Dar al-Tiba'a al-'Amira, 1293.

-------. *Jam' al-Wasa'il fi Sharh al-Shama'il*. A commentary on Tirmidhi's *al-Shama'il*. Cairo, 1317H.

-------. *Mirqat al-Mafatih Sharh Mishkat al-Masabih*. 5 vols. Ed. Muhammad al-Zuhri al-Ghamrawi. Cairo: al-Matba'a al-Maymuniyya, 1309H. Reprint Beirut: Dar Ihya' al-Turath al-'Arabi, n.d.

-------. *Sharh Sharh Nukhba al-Fikar*. A supercommentary on Ibn Hajar's *Sharh Nukhba al-Fikar*. Ed. Muhammad and Haytham Nizar Tamim. Beirut: Dar al-Arqam, n.d.

Al-Saqqaf, Hasan 'Ali. *Sahih Sharh al-'Aqida al-Tahawiyya*. Amman: Dar al-Imam al-Nawawi, 1995.

Al-Shafi'i. *Al-Risala*. Ed. Ahmad Muhammad Shakir. Cairo: n.p., 1939.

Shatta, Ibrahim al-Dusuqi. *Sira al-Shaykh al-Kabir Abi 'Abd Allah Muhammad ibn Khafif al-Shirazi*. Cairo: al-Hay'a al-'Amma li Shu'un al-Matabi' al-Amiriyya, 1977.

Al-Sulami. *Tabaqat al-Sufiyya*. Ed. Nur al-Din Shurayba. Aleppo: Dar al-Kitab al-Nafis, 1986. Reprint of the 1953 edition.

Al-Suyuti. *Al-La'ali' al-Masnu'a fi al-Ahadith al-Mawdu'a*. 2 vols. Beirut: Dar al-Ma'rifa, 1983.

-------. *Sharh Sunan al-Nasa'i*. 9 vols. Ed. 'Abd al-Fattah Abu Ghudda. Aleppo & Beirut: Maktab al-Matbu'at al-Islamiyya, 1986. Includes al-Nasa'is' *Sunan*.

-------, 'Abd al-Ghani al-Dihlawi, and Fakhr al-Hasan al-Gangohi. *Sharh Sunan Ibn Majah*. Karachi: Qadimi Kutub Khana, n.d. Includes Ibn Majah's *Sunan*.

Al-Tabarani. *Al-Mu'jam al-Awsat*. 2 vols. Ed. Mahmud al-Tahhan. Riyadh: Maktaba al-Ma'arif, 1985.

-------. *Al-Mu'jam al-Kabir*. 20 vols. Ed. Hamdi ibn 'Abd al-Majid al-Salafi. Mosul: Maktaba al-'Ulum wa al-Hikam, 1983.

-------. *Al-Mu'jam al-Saghir*. 2 vols. Ed. Muhammad Shakur Mahmud. Beirut and Amman: Al-Maktab al-Islami, Dar 'Ammar, 1985.

-------. *Musnad al-Shamiyyin*. 2 vols. Ed. Hamdi ibn 'Abd al-Majid al-Salafi. Beirut: Mu'assasa al-Risala, 1984.

Al-Tirmidhi. *Sunan*. See al-Mubarakfuri, *Tuhfa al-Ahwadhi*.

SHAYKH MUHYI AL-DIN
IBN 'ARABI
(D. 638)

ISLAMIC
DOCTRINE
('AQÎDA AHL AL-ISLÂM)

Translation and Notes by
Gibril Fouad Haddad

Damascus
1419/1999

This work is humbly dedicated to

**Sultan al-Awliya' Mu'ayyid al-Din wa al-Sunna
Mawlana al-Shaykh Muhammad Nazim Adil
al-Qubrusi al-Naqshbandi al-Haqqani,**

to his Deputy
Shaykh Muhammad Hisham Kabbani,

and to their friends and followers worldwide.

**❲Lo! Verily on Allah's friends is no fear, nor shall they
grieve❳** (10:67)

"I have observed that Ibn 'Arabi's *'Aqida* is, from beginning to
end, the *'Aqida* of the Shaykh Abu al-Hasan al-Ash'ari
without the least difference."
Imam al-Safadi, *al-Wafi bi al-Wafayat.*

"This is my witness in my own regard, and it is the responsibility
of each and every person that it reaches, to bring it forward
if asked about it, whenever and wherever he may be."
Ibn 'Arabi, *'Aqida* §179.

Contents

Shaykh Muhyi al-Din Ibn 'Arabi (d. 638)

Muhammad ibn 'Ali ibn Muhammad ibn al-'Arabi, Abu Bakr Muhyi al-Din al-Hatimi al-Ta'i al-Andalusi al-Mursi al-Dimashqi, known as Ibn 'Arabi to differentiate him from Abu Bakr Ibn al-'Arabi the Maliki jurist. A scholar of Arabic letters at first, then *tafsîr* and *tasawwuf,* nicknamed al-Qushayri and *Sultan al-'Arifîn* in his time for his pre-eminence in *tasawwuf,* known in his lifetime for his devoutness to worship, asceticism, and generosity, Ibn 'Arabi was praised by al-Munawi as "a righteous friend of Allah and a faithful scholar of knowledge" *(waliyyun sâlihun wa 'âli-mun nâsih),* by Ibn 'Imad al-Hanbali as "the absolute *mujta-hid* without doubt," and by al-Fayruzabadi as "the Imam of the People of *Shari'a* both in knowledge and in legacy, the educator of the People of the Way in practice and in knowledge, and the shaykh of the shaykhs of the People of Truth through spiritual experience *(dhawq)* and understanding."[1]

His Teachers

He travelled East and West in the study of hadith, taking knowledge from over a thousand shaykhs, among them Abu al-Hasan ibn Hudhayl, Muhammad ibn Khalaf al-Lakhmi, Ibn Zarqun, Abu al-Walid al-Hadrami, al-Silafi, 'Abd al-Haqq al-Ishbili, Ibn 'Asakir, Ibn al-Jawzi, and Ibn Bushku-wal. His principal shaykhs in *tasawwuf* were Abu Madyan al-Maghribi, Jamal al-Din Yunus ibn Yahya al-Qassar, Abu 'Abd Allah al-Tamimi al-Fasi, Abu al-Hasan ibn Jami', and al-Khidr 🕮.[2] He became known first as *al-Shaykh al-Kabir*

---

[1] In al-Qari, *Firr al-'Awn* (p. 141-142).
[2] Ibn al-Jawzi in his book *'Ujala al-Muntazir fi Sharh Hal al-Khadir* expressed the extreme view that to suggest that al-Khidr is alive

("The Great Shaykh") then *al-Shaykh al-Akbar* ("The Greatest Shaykh") with specific reference to the sciences of *tasawwuf* in which he authored hundreds of books.[3]

His Doctrine *('Aqîda)*

His greatest and best-known is his last work, *al-Futuhat al-Makkiyya* ("The Meccan Conquests") which begins with a statement of doctrine – translated in the present volume – about which al-Safadi said: "I saw that from beginning to end it consists in the doctrine of Abu al-Hasan al-Ash'ari without any difference whatsoever."[4]

His Rank of *Mujtahid Mutlaq*

In jurisprudence Ibn 'Arabi is often said to follow the Zahiri school, but this is incorrect since he himself denies it,

---

contradicts the *Shari'a*. Ibn 'Ata' Allah in *Lata'if al-Minan* (1:84-98) flatly rejected this and showed that there is consensus among the Sufis that al-Khidr is alive. For the opposite view see Ibn al-Qayyim, *al-Manar al-Munif* (p. 67-76) with 'Abd al-Fattah Abu Ghudda's comprehensive notes. The hadith master al-Sakhawi stated: "It is well-known that al-Nawawi used to meet with Khidr and converse with him among many other unveilings *(mukâshafât)*." Al-Sakhawi, *Tarjima Shaykh al-Islam Qutb al-Awliya' al-Kiram wa Faqih al-Anam Muhyi al-Sunna wa Mumit al-Bid'a Abi Zakariyya Muhyi al-Din al-Nawawi* ("Biography of the Shaykh of Islam, the Pole of the Noble Saints and Jurist of Mankind, the Reviver of the Sunna and Slayer of Innovation Abu Zakariyya Muhyiddin al-Nawawi") (Cairo: Jam'iyya al-Nashr wa al-Ta'lif al-Azhariyya, 1354/1935 p. 33).

[3]See Hilmi's 284-entry bibliography in *al-Burhan al-Azhar* as well as the books of Prof. Michel Chodkiewicz (*The Seal of Saints* and *An Ocean Without Shore*) and his daughter Prof. Claude Addas *(Quest for the Red Sulphur)*.

[4]In al-Suyuti, *Tanbih al-Ghabi* (p. 71).

as quoted by Ibn 'Imad from Ibn 'Arabi's two poems *al-Ra'iyya* and *al-Nuniyya*, which state respectively:

> *Laqad harrama al-Rahmânu taqlîda Mâlikin*
> *wa Ahmada wa al-Nu'mani wa al-kulli fa'dhurû*

The Merciful forbade me to imitate Malik, Ahmad,
Al-Nu'man [Abu Hanifa] and others, therefore pardon me.

> *Lastu mimman yaqûlu qâla Ibnu Hazmin*
> *lâ wa lâ Ahmadu wa la al-Nu'mânu*

I am not of those who say: "Ibn Hazm said"—
Certainly not! Nor "Ahmad said" nor "al-Nu'man said."[5]

The Controversy Surrounding Him

The name of Ibn 'Arabi remains associated with controversy because of those who criticized him severely for the work attributed to him under the title *Fusûs al-Hikam* ("The Precious Stones of the Wisdoms"). The attribution of this work in its present form to Ibn 'Arabi is undoubtedly incorrect as the *Fusûs* contradicts some of the most basic tenets of Islam expounded by Ibn 'Arabi himself in his authentic works, such as the finality of Prophethood, the primacy of Prophets over non-Prophets, the abrogation of all religious creeds other than Islam, the everlastingness of the punishment of Hellfire and its dwellers, the abiding therein of anyone that does not accept the Prophet ﷺ after his coming, Pharaoh's damnation, etc. Nevertheless the *Fusûs* have received commentaries by the following scholars among others: Sadr al-Din al-Qunawi (d. 671), 'Afif al-Din al-

---

[5]In Ibn 'Imad, *Shadharat al-Dhahab* (5:200).

Tilimsani (d. 690), Mu'ayyid al-Din al-Jundi (d. 700), Sa'd al-Din al-Farghani (d. 700), Kamal al-Din al-Zamalkani (d. 727), Dawud al-Qaysari (d. 751), Kamal al-Din al-Qashani (d. 751), Sayyid 'Ali al-Hamadani (d. 766), Khwaja Muhammad Parsa (d. 822) the intimate friend of Shah Naqshband ﷺ, Mawlana Jami (d. 898), Isma'il al-Anqarawi (d. 1042), 'Abd al-Ghani al-Nabulusi (d. 1144), and others.

Al-Suyuti's Response to al-Biqa'i

In response to an attack by Burhan al-Din al-Biqa'i (d. 885) entitled *Tanbih al-Ghabi ila Takfir Ibn 'Arabi wa Tahdhir al-'Ibad min Ahl al-'Inad* ("Warning to the Ignoramus Concerning the Declaration of Ibn 'Arabi's Disbelief, and Cautioning Allah's Servants Against Stubborn People") Sayyid 'Ali ibn Maymun al-Maghribi (d. 917) wrote a fatwa entitled *Tanbih al-Ghabi fi Tanzih Ibn 'Arabi* ("Warning to the Ignoramus Concerning Ibn 'Arabi's Vindication"). Al-Suyuti wrote a fatwa with the same title, in which he stated:

> The scholars past and present have differed concerning Ibn 'Arabi, one group considering him a friend of Allah *(wali)* – and they are correct – such as Ibn 'Ata' Allah al-Sakandari and 'Afif al-Din al-Yafi'i, another considering him a heretic – such as a large number of the jurists – while others expressed doubts concerning him, among them al-Dhahabi in *al-Mizan*. Two opposed verdicts are reported from Shaykh 'Izz al-Din ibn 'Abd al-Salam, one attacking him, and one describing him as the Spiritual Pole *(al-qutb)*. What reconciles them is indicated by Shaykh Taj al-Din ibn 'Ata' Allah in *Lata'if al-Minan* [*fi Manaqib Abi al-'Abbas al-Mursi wa Shaykhihi Abi al-Hasan al-Shadhili*], namely, that Shaykh 'Izz al-Din at the

6

beginning acted in the fashion of jurists in passing quick judgment on the Sufis. When Shaykh Abu al-Hasan al-Shadhili went to pilgrimage and returned, he came to Shaykh 'Izz al-Din before entering his own house and conveyed to him the Prophet's 鑗 greeting. After that, Shaykh 'Izz al-Din humbled himself and began to sit in al-Shadhili's gatherings....[6] Our shaykh, Shaykh al-Islam, the last remnant of the *mujtahid*s, Sharaf al-Din al-Munawi replied, concerning Ibn 'Arabi, that silence was safest. And this is the stance that befits every truly Godwary person who fears for himself. For me, the last word concerning Ibn 'Arabi – and this is accepted neither by his contemporary admirers nor by his detractors – is that he be considered a *walî*, but reading his books is forbidden.[7]

Whatever is transmitted and attributed to the [Sufi] Shaykhs – may Allah be well pleased with them – if it contradicts external knowledge, bears various possibilities:

First, we do not concede its attribution to them until it is established as authentic.

Second, after authenticity is established, it may have a figurative meaning; if not, then one should say: "Perhaps it has a figurative meaning for the people of internal knowledge and the knowers of Allah Almighty."

Third, this may have come from them in a state of intoxication and distraction, and the lawfully intoxicated

---

[6]Cf. al-Suyuti's *Tanbih al-Ghabi* (p. 52-54).
[7]Al-Suyuti, *Tanbih al-Ghabi fi Takhti'a Ibn 'Arabi* (p. 17-21). The correct title has *tanzih* instead of *takhti'a* as in Hajji Khalifa's *Kashf al-Zunun* (1:488) and al-Qari's works.

person is not taken to task as he is not held responsible in such a state.

Holding a bad opinion about them after all these resolutions is a sign of deprivement of success. We seek refuge in Allah from failure and a terrible verdict, and from all evils![8]

Ibn 'Arabi's Admirers

Al-Suyuti's attitude and what he reports from al-Munawi is echoed by Imam al-Safadi who said of Ibn 'Arabi: "He was a very great man, and whatever can be understood from his words is excellent and upright; as for what we find difficult, we leave its matter to Allah, for we were not tasked with following him nor with doing all that he said."[9] Similarly al-Qari admitted in one of his fatwas against Ibn 'Arabi and his works: "The safest course in Religion concerning the person of Ibn 'Arabi is silence, as the scholars differed about him."[10]

The hadith master Ibn al-Najjar (d. 643) wrote a long notice on him in his biographical history in which he said: "I met him in Damascus and copied some of his poetry. What a wonderful shaykh he was!"[11] Among the famous authorities who held a good opinion of Ibn 'Arabi are the following:

- The Qur'anic commentator and jurist Imam al-Baydawi who called him "the Imam of Verification in reality and outwardly";

---

[8]Al-Suyuti, *Tanbih al-Ghabi* (p. 59-60).
[9]In al-Suyuti, *Tanbih al-Ghabi* (p. 70).
[10]Al-Qari, *Risala fi Wahda al-Shuhud* (p. 62).
[11]Ibn al-Najjar, *Dhayl Tarikh Baghdad* as quoted in al-Suyuti, *Tanbih al-Ghabi* (p. 64-66) and in Ibn Hajar, *Lisan al-Mizan* (5:311 #1038).

8

- The Qur'anic commentator Abu al-Su'ud;

- Imam al-Safadi the author of *al-Wafi bi al-Wafayat*;[12]

- Zayn al-Din al-Khafi al-Akbar Abadi;[13]

- Ibn 'Imad al-Hanbali who called him "the Great Knower of Allah" *(al-'ârif al-kabîr)*;[14]

- Kamal al-Din 'Abd al-Wahid ibn 'Abd al-Karim Ibn al-Zamalkani (d. 651) who called him "the Ocean replete with all kinds of divine knowledges";

- Safi al-Din al-Azdi al-Ansari in his epistle on the scholars of his time;

- Shaykh Jalal al-Din al-Dawani (d. 907);[15]

- Majd al-Din al-Shirazi al-Siddiqi in his fatwa entitled *al-Ightibat bi Mu'alaja Ibn al-Khayyat*;[16]

- Al-Sayyid al-Jurjani whose *Ta'rifat* include Ibn 'Arabi's terminologies;

- The lexicographer, hadith scholar and jurist al-Fayruzabadi who in his commentary on al-Bukhari's *Sahih* often quotes Ibn 'Arabi's explanations;

- Imam al-Yafi'i who called him in his *Tarikh* "the Paragon of Allah's Friends in knowledge and *fiqh* outwardly and inwardly";

- *Qadi al-Qudat* Shams al-Din al-Bisati al-Maliki who opposed before the Sultan – in Ibn Hajar's presence –

---

[12] As related from al-Biqa'i by al-Suyuti in *Tanbih al-Ghabi* (p. 40-41).
[13] As related from al-Biqa'i by al-Suyuti in *Tanbih al-Ghabi* (p. 42-43).
[14] In *Shadharat al-Dhahab* (5:190).
[15] Al-Qari wrote *Firr al-'Awn* in reply to him.
[16] Al-Qari addresses it towards the end of *Firr al-'Awn* (p. 142f.).

'Ala' al-Din al-Bukhari's verdict of *takfir* of Ibn 'Arabi and whoever accepted him;[17]

• *Shaykh al-Islam* Siraj al-Din al-Makhzumi who said: "Our shaykh, *Shaykh al-Islam* Siraj al-Din al-Bulqini and likewise Shaykh Taqi al-Din al-Subki used to criticize the Shaykh in the beginning, then they changed their position after they realized what he was saying and the explanation of his intent."[18]

• Al-Bulqini who was reported by his student al-Makhzumi as saying: "We seek refuge in Allah from saying that he [Ibn 'Arabi] affirms indwelling *(hulûl)* and communion-with-the-divine *(ittihâd)*! He is far above that. Rather, he is one of the greatest imams and among those who have probed the oceans of the sciences of the Book and the Sunna."[19]

• *Shaykh al-Islam* Zakariyya al-Ansari in the chapter of apostasy in his book *Sharh Kitab al-Rawd fi al-Fiqh wa al-Fatwa*;

• *Shaykh al-Islam* al-Haytami in his *Fatawa Hadithiyya*;

• Imam Shams al-Din Muhammad al-Bakri;

• The hadith master and Qur'anic commentator Shaykh Isma'il Haqqi in his book *al-Khitab*;

• The Ottoman writer Katib Çelebi who devoted a chapter on him in his book *Mizan al-Haqq fi Ikhtyar al-Ahaqq*;

• Shaykh Mulla al-Jami in *Nafahat al-Uns*;

---

[17]See Ibn Hajar, *Inba' al-Ghumr bi A'mar al-'Umr* (3:403-404), year 831.
[18]In Hilmi, *al-Burhan al-Azhar* (p. 32-33).
[19]*Ibid.* (p. 34).

- The hadith master of Damascus and Renewer of the Thirteenth Islamic century, Shaykh Badr al-Din al-Hasani;[20]

- Sayyid Jamal al-Din al-Qasimi in his *Qawa'id al-Tahdith*;[21]

- *Shaykh al-Islam* al-Munawi who cited him over two hundred times in *Fayd al-Qadir* and elsewhere declared:

> A group of scholars professed suspension of judgment *(waqf)* and benefit of good opinion *(al-taslîm)*... their Imam being Shaykh al-Islam al-Nawawi who replied, when asked about Ibn 'Arabi: **❨Those are a people who have passed away. Theirs is that which they earned, and yours is that which you earn. And you will not be asked of what they used to do❩** (2:134). [The Maliki Imam Ahmad] Zarruq reported from his shaykh al-Nuri the words: "They differed about him from the verdict of disbelief to that of spiritual primacy *(qutbâniyya)*, and giving the benefit of good opinion is therefore an obligation."[22]

Wahda al-Wujûd or Oneness of Being

Perhaps the most famous misrepresentation of the Shaykh that resulted from the *Fusûs* is the attribution to him of the doctrine of "oneness of being" *(wahda al-wujûd)* in the

---

[20]As narrated from Mr. Orfan Rabbat from his grandson Muhammad Badr al-Din. On Shaykh Badr al-Din al-Hasani see the biography by his student Shaykh Mahmud al-Rankusi entitled *al-Durar al-Lu'lu'iyya fî al-Nu'ut al-Badriyya* (Damascus, 1951).
[21]Al-Qasimi, *Qawa'id al-Tahdith* (p. 348-351).
[22]In Ibn 'Imad, *Shadharat al-Dhahab* (5:192).

pantheistic sense of the immanence of the Deity in everything that exists. Al-Qari cites, for example, a verse of poetry which he references to the *Fusûs*, stating:

Subhâna man azhara al-ashyâ'a wa huwa 'aynuhâ
Glory to Him Who caused things to appear
and is those very things![23]

This attribution and others of its type are evidently spurious, and Ibn 'Arabi's *'Aqida* flatly contradicts them. Furthermore, verifying scholars such as Shaykh Ahmad Sirhindi in his epistles, Shaykh 'Abd al-Ghani al-Nabulusi in *al-Radd al-Matin 'ala Muntaqid al-'Arif Billah Muhyi al-Din* and *Idah al-Maqsud min Wahda al-Wujud,* and al-Sha'rani in *al-Yawaqit wa al-Jawahir* and *Tanbih al-Aghbiya' 'ala Qatratin min Bahri 'Ulum al-Awliya* have rephrased Ibn 'Arabi's expression of "oneness of being" *(wahda al-wujûd)* as "oneness of perception" *(wahda al-shuhûd)* in the sense in which the Prophet ﷺ defined excellence *(ihsân)* as "worshipping Allah as if you see Him."[24] Al-Buti said:

> What is the meaning of the expression "oneness of perception"? When I interact with causes with full respect to Allah's ways, His orders, and His Law, knowing that the sustenance that comes to me is from Allah; the felicity that enters my home is from Allah Almighty; my food is readied for me by Allah – I mean even the smallest details; the wealth with which I have been graced, comes from Allah; the illness that has been put in my being or that of a relative of mine comes from Allah Almighty; the

---

[23]In al-Qari, *Risala fi Wahda al-Shuhud* (p. 55).
[24]Narrated from Abu Hurayra by Bukhari, Muslim, Ahmad, al-Nasa'i, and Ibn Majah; from 'Umar by Muslim, al-Tirmidhi, Abu Dawud, Ibn Majah, Ahmad, and al-Nasa'i; and from Abu Dharr by al-Nasa'i, all as part of a longer hadith.

cure that followed it is from Allah Almighty; my success in my studies is by Allah Almighty's grant; the results which I have attained after obtaining my degrees and so forth, are from Allah Almighty's grant – when the efficacy of causes melts away in my sight and I no longer see, behind them, other than the Causator Who is Allah Almighty: at that time, when you look right, you do not see except Allah's Attributes, and when you look left, you do not see other than Allah's Attributes. As much as you evolve in the world of causes, you do not see, through them, other than the Causator, Who is Allah. At that time you have become raised to what the spiritual masters have called oneness of perception. And this oneness of perception is what Allah's Messenger ﷺ expressed by the word *ihsân* [which he defined to mean]: "That you worship Allah as if you see him." You do not see the causes as a barrier between you and Allah. Rather, you see causes, in the context of this doctrine, very much like pure, transparent glass: the glass pane is present – no one denies it – but as much as you stare at it, you do not see anything except what is behind it. Is it not so? You only see what is behind it. The world is entirely made of glass panes in this fashion. You see in them Allah's efficacy in permanence, so you are always with Allah Almighty. None has tasted the sweetness of belief unless he has reached that level of perception.[25]

Ibn Taymiyya's Unreliability

Ibn Taymiyya is quoted in his *Fatawa* as being asked repeatedly about "the verdict of Islam concerning Ibn 'Arabi

---

[25]From Dr. Sa'id al-Buti's unpublished commentary on Ibn 'Ata' Allah's *Hikam*.

who asserted Oneness of Being," and other similar questions. However, it seems that Ibn Taymiyya did not review the Shaykh's huge *Futuhat* in its totality when he answered these questions. At times, his discussions about Ibn 'Arabi depend, as he puts it, on "whether these are his actual words" while at other times he attacks him outright on the basis of these unverified assumptions, or himself levels specific accusations against the Shaykh. Muhammad Ghurab – a contemporary authority on Ibn 'Arabi's works – in a book published in the 1980s by Dar al-Fikr in Damascus, states having read the *Futuhat* several times from cover to cover without finding the expressions for which Ibn Taymiyya took the Shaykh to task while citing this work. The late hadith scholar of Damascus Shaykh Mahmud al-Rankusi similarly affirmed that Ibn Taymiyya answered questions about Ibn 'Arabi without confirming them against his actual writings, and that the sharp temper of the former further complicated his attitude towards the Shaykh. On the basis of these opinions and in the light of Ibn Taymiyya's occasional reservations and his otherwise apparently correct approach to ambiguous expressions, it seems that the misquotations of Ibn 'Arabi became so numerous in Ibn Taymiyya's time that it became inconceivable to him that they were all incorrect, whereupon he treated them as facts. The errors causing these misquotations can also be inferred from the fact that since the misquotations revolved around issues of doctrine – in which misunderstandings are fraught with grave dangers – and in light of the Shaykh's complex style and obscure expressions, queries would be commonly sent to muftis concerning what some people *thought* they had read, without actually citing nor understanding the expressions in question. All this could have been avoided by the due observance of faithfulness *(amâna)* in textual citation, as the early scholars insisted with reference to hadith transmission. Yet many later scholars, beginning with Ibn Taymiyya and after him, relied on second and third-hand paraphrases and attributions, endorsing the accusations against Ibn 'Arabi and even generalizing them so as to target all *tasawwuf*. Finally, Ibn Taymiyya in his letter to al-Munayji actually states his admiration for the *Futuhat* and reserves his criticism only for the *Fusûs!*[26]

Other Critics of Ibn 'Arabi

Among the scholars cited by al-Qari as condemning Ibn 'Arabi as an innovator or even an outright heretic *(zindîq)* and disbeliever because of *Fusûs al-Hikam*: Ibn 'Abd al-Salam, al-Jazari, Sharaf al-Din ibn al-Muqri, Abu Hayyan al-Andalusi, Sa'd al-Din al-Taftazani,[27] Jamal al-Din Muhammad ibn Nur al-Din,[28] Siraj al-Din al-Bulqini who

---

[26]"I was one of those who, previously, used to hold the best opinion of Ibn 'Arabi and extol his praise, because of the benefits I saw in his books, such as *al-Futuhat, al-Kanh, al-Muhkam al-Marbut, al-Durra al-Fakhira, Matali' al-Nujum,* and other such works." Ibn Taymiyya, *Tawhid al-Rububiyya* in *Majmu'a al-Fatawa* (2:464-465).

[27]In his epistle entitled *Risala fî Wahda al-Wujud,* a title also used by al-Qari. Al-Taftazani was answered by the Hanafi jurist Isma'il Kalnabawi in a fatwa cited in full in *al-Burhan al-Azhar* (p. 18-22).

[28]As named by al-Qari in his *Risala fî Wahda al-Wujud* (p. 61).

supposedly ordered his books burnt,[29] Burhan al-Din al-Biqa'i, Ibn Taymiyya,[30] and his student al-Dhahabi who said:

He may well have been one of Allah's Friends Whom He strongly attracted to Himself upon death and for whom He sealed a good ending. As for his words, whoever understands them, recognizes them to be on the bases of communion-with-the-divine *(ittihâdiyya)*, knowing the deviation of those people and comprehending theirs expressions: the truth will be apparent to him as against what they say.[31]

The Hanafi shaykh 'Ala' al-Din al-Bukhari, like Ibn al-Muqri, went so far as to declare anyone who did not declare Ibn 'Arabi a disbeliever to be himself a disbeliever. This is the same 'Ala' al-Din al-Bukhari who said that anyone that gives Ibn Taymiyya the title *Shaykh al-Islam* is a disbeliever.

---

[29] In al-Qari, *Firr al-'Awn* (p. 144). Al-Fayruzabadi said: "If the report whereby Ibn 'Abd al-Salam and our shaykh al-Bulqini ordered Ibn 'Arabi's books burnt were true, not one of his books would have remained today in Egypt or *Sham*, and no-one would have dared copy them again after the words of these two shaykhs." In Hilmi, *al-Burhan al-Azhar* (p. 32). Al-Hilmi adds (p. 34) that a further proof that al-Subki changed his position concerning Ibn 'Arabi is that he wrote many refutations against the heresies of his time but never wrote against Ibn 'Arabi, although his books were widely read in Damascus and elsewhere.

[30] He wrote *al-Radd al-Aqwam 'ala ma fi Fusûs al-Hikam* but is on record as not objecting to Ibn 'Arabi's other works, as showed.

[31] *Mizan al-I'tidal* (3:660). Al-Dhahabi in the same chapter makes derogatory comments and reports a strange story which Ibn Hajar cited in *Lisan al-Mizan*. Al-Qari also attributes negative comments on Ibn 'Arabi to al-Suyuti in the latter's *al-Tahbir li 'Ilm al-Tafsir* and *Itmam al-Diraya Sharh al-Niqaya*.

Al-Haytami's Response

Al-Haytami said in his *Fatawa Hadithiyya*:

Our shaykh [Zakariyya al-Ansari] said in *Sharh al-Rawd...* in response to Ibn al-Muqri's statement: "Whoever doubts in the disbelief *(kufr)* of Ibn 'Arabi's group, he himself is a disbeliever":

The truth is that Ibn 'Arabi and his group are the elite of the *Umma*. Al-Yafi'i, Ibn 'Ata' Allah and others have declared that they considered Ibn 'Arabi a *walî*, noting that the language which Sufis use is appropriate among the experts in its usage and that the knower of Allah *('ârif)*, when he becomes completely absorbed in the oceans of Unity, might make some statements that are liable to be misconstrued as indwelling *(hulûl)* and union *(ittihâd)*, while in reality there is neither indwelling nor union.

It has been clearly stated by our Imams, such as al-Rafi'i in his book *al-'Aziz*, al-Nawawi in *al-Rawda and al-Majmu'*, and others:

When a mufti is being asked about a certain phrase that could be construed as disbelief, he should not immediately say that the speaker should be put to death nor make permissible the shedding of his blood. Rather let him say: The speaker must be asked about what he meant by his statement, and

17

he should hear his explanation, then act
accordingly.[32]

Look at these guidelines – may Allah guide you! –
and you will find that the deniers who assault this great
man (Ibn 'Arabi) and positively assert his disbelief, are

---

[32]Al-Khadimi wrote in the introduction to his *Sharh Ma'ani al-
Basmala*: "It was stated in *al-Bazaziyya* that if a certain question has a
hundred aspects, ninety-nine of which entail disbelief and one
precludes it, the scholar must lean towards the latter and not give a
fatwa to the apostasy of a Muslim as long as he can give his words a
good interpretation. Also, in *al-Usul*: No preference is given in the face
of abundant evidence to the contrary." As cited in *al-Burhan al-Azhar*
(p. 17-18). In *Bustan al-'Arifin* al-Nawawi states, after reporting Abu
al-Khayr al-Tibyani's apparent breach of the *Shari'a*: "Someone that
imitates jurists without understanding may imagine wrong and object
to this, out of ignorance and stupidity. To imagine wrong here is plain
recklessness in giving vent to suspicions against the Friends of the All-
Merciful. The wise person must beware from such behavior! On the
contrary, if one did not understand the wisdoms from which they
benefited and their fine subtleties, it is his duty is to understand them
from one who does. You may witness such occurrences about which
the superficial person gets the illusion of deviation, but which are
actually not deviant. On the contrary, it is obligatory to interpret
figuratively the actions of Allah's friends." As cited in al-Suyuti's
Tanbih al-Ghabi (p. 45-46) and Ibn 'Imad, *Shadharat al-Dhahab*
(5:194). The rules spelled out by al-Nawawi, al-Haytami, and al-
Khadimi refute the presumption that only the statements of the Prophet
 may be interpreted figuratively (cf. al-Qunawi in al-Qari's *Risala fi
Wahda al-Wujud* p. 110 and al-Suyuti's *Tanbih al-Ghabi* p. 44-45, as
against 'Ala' al-Din al-Bukhari in al-Qari's *Firr al-'Awn* p. 153; cf. al-
Munawi in Ibn 'Imad, *Shadharat* 5:194) or that "every truth that
contravenes the outward rule of the Law consists in disguised disbelief
(zandaqa)" (al-Qari, *Firr al-'Awn* p. 152). The most shining refutation
of the latter claim lies in the Prophet's hadith of the straying desert
traveller who, finding his mount and provisions after having lost them,
is so overwhelmed by joy that he exclaims: "O Allah, You are my
slave and I am Your master!" Narrated from Anas by Muslim in his
Sahih.

riding upon blind mounts, and stumbling about like a camel affected with troubled vision. Verily Allah has blocked their sight and hearing from perceiving this, until they fell into whatever they fell into, which caused them to be despised, and made their knowledge of no benefit. The great knowledge of the Sufis and their utter renunciation of this world and of everything other than Allah testify to their innocence from these terrible accusations, therefore we prefer to dismiss such accusations and consider that their statements are true realities in the way they expressed them. Their way cannot be denied without knowing the meaning of their statements and the expressions they use, and then turning to apply the expression to the meaning and see if they match or not. We thank Allah that all of their deniers are ignorant in that kind of knowledge, as not one of them has mastered the sciences of unveilings *(mukâshafât)*, nor even smelled them from a distance! Nor has anyone of them sincerely followed any of the *awliyâ'* so as to master their terminology.

You may object: "I disagree that their expressions refer to a reality rather than being metaphorical phrases, therefore show me something clearer than the explanations that have been given." I say: Rejection is stubborness. Let us assume that you disagree with what I have mentioned, but the correct way of stating the objection is to say: "This statement could be interpreted in several ways," and proceed to explain them. You should not say: "If it meant this, then... and if it meant that, then..." while stating from the start "This is *kufr*"! That is ignorance and goes beyond the scope of sincere faithfulness *(nasîha)* claimed by the critic.

19

Do you not see that if Ibn al-Muqri's real motivation were good advice, he would not have exaggerated by saying: "Whoever has a doubt in the disbelief of the group of Ibn 'Arabi, he himself is a disbeliever"? So he extended his judgment that Ibn 'Arabi's followers were disbelievers, to everyone who had a doubt as to their disbelief. Look at this fanaticism that exceeds all bounds and departs from the consensus of the Imams, and goes so far as to accuse anyone who doubts their disbelief. **❲Glorified are You, this is awful calumny❳** (24:16) **❲When you welcomed it with your tongues, and uttered with your mouths that whereof you had no knowledge, you counted it a trifle. In the sight of Allah, it is very great❳** (24:15).

Notice also that his statement suggests that it is an obligation on the whole Community to believe that Ibn 'Arabi and his followers are disbelievers, otherwise they will all be declared disbelievers – and no one thinks likes this. As a matter of fact, it might well lead into something forbidden which he himself has stated clearly in his book *al-Rawd* when he said: "Whoever accuses a Muslim of being a disbeliever based on a sin committed by him, and without an attempt to interpret it favorably, he himself commits disbelief." Yet here he is accusing an entire group of Muslims of disbelief.[33] Moreover, no consideration should be paid to his interpretation, because he only gives the kind of interpretation that is detrimental to those he is criticizing, for that is all that their words have impressed upon him.

---

[33] Al-Sakhawi in *al-Daw' al-Lami'* similarly points out this contradiction between al-Biqa'i's expressed principles and his actual practices.

As for those who do not think of Ibn 'Arabi and the Sufis except as a pure light in front of them, and believe in their sainthood – how can a Muslim attack them by accusing them of disbelief? No one would dare do so unless he is accepting the possibility to be himself called a disbeliever. This judgment reflects a great deal of fanaticism, and an assault on most of the Muslims. We ask Allah, through His Mercy, to forgive the one who uttered it.

It has been narrated through more than one source and has become well-known to everyone that whoever opposes the Sufis, Allah will not make His Knowledge beneficial, and he will be inflicted with the worst and ugliest diseases. We have witnessed this taking place with many naysayers. For example, al-Biqa'i – may Allah forgive him! – used to be one of the most distinguished scholars, blessed with many meritorious acts of worship, an exceptional intelligence, and an excellent memory in all kinds of knowledge, especially in the sciences of *tafsîr* and hadith, and he wrote numerous books, but Allah did not allow them to be of any kind of benefit to anyone. He also authored a book called *Munasabat al-Qur'an* in about ten volumes, about which no-one knows except the elite, and as for the rest, they never heard about it. If this book had been written by our Shaykh Zakariyya [al-Ansari], or by anyone who believes [in *awliyâ'*], it would have been copied with gold because, as a matter of fact, it has no equal: for **❴Of the bounties of thy Lord We bestow freely on all, these as well as those: the bounties of thy Lord are not closed to anyone❵** (17:20).

Al-Biqa'i went to extremes in his denial and wrote books about the subject, all of them clearly and excessively fanatical and deviating from the straight path.

21

But then he paid for it fully and even more than that, for he was caught in the act on several occasions and was judged a disbeliever. It was ruled that his blood be shed and he was about to get killed, but he asked the help and protection of some influential people who rescued him, and he was made to repent in Salihiyya, Egypt, and renew his Islam.[34]

Al-Dhahabi's Warning to Critics of Sufis

Al-Dhahabi voiced something similar to al-Haytami's warnings against those inclined to attack Sufis:

> Our Shaykh Ibn Wahb [= Ibn Daqiq al-'Id] said – may Allah have mercy on him: 'Among the predicaments that mar the discipline of narrator-discreditation are the divergences that take place between the followers of *tasawwuf (al-mutasawwifa)* and the people of external knowledge *(ahl al-'ilm al-zâhir)*; animosity therefore arose between these two groups and necessitated mutual criticism.'

> Now this [animosity against Sufis] is a plunge from which none escapes unscathed except one thoroughly knowledgeable with all the evidentiary proofs of the Law. Note that I do not limit such knowledge to the branches [of the Law]. For, concerning many of the states described by the people of truth *(al-muhiqqîn)* among the Sufis, right cannot be told from wrong on the mere basis of knowledge of the branches.

---

[34] Al-Haytami, *Fatawa Hadithiyya* (p. 331). For the account of the condemnation of al-Biqa'i himself as a *kâfir* see al-Sakhawi's *al-Daw' al-Lami'* and al-Shawkani's *al-Badr al-Tali'*.

One must also possess firm knowledge of the principles of the Law and be able to tell apart the obligatory from the possible, as well as the rationally impossible from the customarily impossible.

It is, indeed, a position fraught with danger! For the critic of a true Sufi *(muhiqq al-sûfiyya)* enters into the hadith: "Whosoever shows enmity to one of My Friends, I shall declare war upon him."[35] While one that abandons all condemnation for what is clearly wrong in what he hears from some of them, abandons the commanding of good and the forbidding of evil.[36]

Some of Ibn 'Arabi's Sayings

It is remarkable that there were very few contemporaries of Ibn 'Arabi among his accusers, although he travelled and taught all over the Islamic world and, as Ibn Hajar stated, "he

---

[35]The complete hadith states: "Whosoever shows enmity to one of My Friends, I shall declare war upon him. My servant draws not near to Me with anything more loved by Me than the religious duties I have enjoined upon him, and My servant continues to draw near to Me with supererogatory works so that I shall love him. When I love him I am his hearing with which he hears, his seeing with which he sees, his hand with which he strikes, his foot with which he walks. Were he to ask something of Me, I would surely give it to him. Were he to seek refuge in Me, I would surely grant him it. Nor do I hesitate to do anything as I hesitate to take back the believer's soul, for he hates death and I hate to hurt him." Narrated from Abu Hurayra by Bukhari. Ibn 'Abd al-Salam in *al-Ishara ila al-Ijaz* (p. 108).said: "Allah's hesitancy' in this hadith is a metaphor of the superlative rank of the believer in Allah's presence and connotes a lesser hurt to prevent a greater harm, as in the case of a father's severance of his son's gangrened hand so as to save his life."
[36]Al-Dhahabi, *al-Muqiza* (p. 88-90).

made his mark in every country that he entered"[37] while his admirers among the authorities of Islam lived both in his own lifetime and later. Among the Shaykh's sayings:

- "Whoever is truthful in something and pursues it diligently will obtain it sooner or later; if he does not obtain it in this world, he will obtain it in the next; and whoever dies before victory shall be elevated to the level of his diligence."

- "The knower of Allah knows through eyesight *(basar)* what others know through insight *(basîra)*, and he knows through insight what virtually no-one knows. Despite this, he does not feel secure from the harm of his ego towards himself; how then could he ever feel secure from what His Lord has foreordained for him?"

- "The knower's declaration to his student: 'Take from me this science which you can find nowhere else,' does not detract from the knower's level, nor do other similar declarations that appear to be self-eulogy, because his intention is only to encourage the student to receive it."

- "The discourse of the knower is in the image of the listener according to the latter's powers, readiness, weakness, and inner reservations."

- "If you find it complicated to answer someone's question, do not answer it, for his container is already full and does not have room for the answer."

- "The ignorant one does not see his ignorance as he basks in its darkness; nor does the knowledgeable one see his own knowledge, for he basks in its light."

---

[37]Ibn Hajar, *Lisan al-Mizan* (5:311 #1038). See also his words in *al-Intisar li A'imma al-Amsar* and in al-Qari's *Risala fi Wahda al-Wujud* (p. 113).

- "Whoever asks for a proof for Allah's oneness, a donkey knows more than him."

His *Tarjuman al-Ashwaq* ("The Interpreter of Desires") is a masterpiece of Arabic poetry translated in many languages. The following poem to the Ka'ba is taken from the *Futuhat*:[a]

1. *In the Place of refuge my heart sought refuge,*
   shot with enmity's arrows.
2. *O Mercy of Allah for His slaves, Allah placed His trust*
   in you among all inanimate forms.
3. *O House of my Lord, O light of my heart,*
   O coolness of my eyes,[b] O my heart within,
4. *O true secret of the heart of existence,*
   my sacred trust, my purest love!
5. *O direction from which I turn from every quarter and*
   valley,
6. *From subsistence in the Real, then from the height,*
   from self-extinction, then from the depths!
7. *O Ka'ba of Allah, O my life,*
   O path of good fortune, O my guidance,
8. *In you has Allah placed every safety*
   from the fear of disaster upon the Return.
9. *In you does the noble Station flourish,*
   in you are found the fortunes of Allah's slaves.
10. *In you is the Right Hand that my sin has draped*
    in the robe of blackness.[c]

---

[a] Ibn 'Arabi, *Futuhat* (original ed. 1:701).
[b] The mere sight of Ka'ba is considered worship.
[c] The hadith "The Black Stone is Allah's right hand" is narrated from Ibn 'Abbas, Jabir, Anas, and others by Ibn Abi 'Umar al-Ma'dani in his *Musnad*, al-Tabarani, al-Suyuti in *al-Jami' al-Saghir* (1:516), Ibn 'Asakir in his *Tarikh* (15:90-92), al-Khatib in his (6:328), and others. Al-'Ajluni stated that it is *sahih* as a halted report from Ibn 'Abbas as narrated by al-Quda'i in the wording: "The Corner is Allah's Right

11. *Multazam is in you – he who clings to love for it,*
    will be saved on the Day of Mutual Cries.[d]
12. *Souls passed away longing for Her,*
    in the pain of longing and distant separation.
13. *In sorrow at their news she has put on*
    the garment of mourning.[e]
14. *Allah sheds His light on her court,*
    and something of His light appears in the heart.
15. *None sees it but the sorrowful*
    whose eyes are dark from lack of sleep.
16. *He circumambulates seven times after seven,*
    from the beginning of night until the call to prayer.
17. *Hostage to endless sadness, he is never seen*
    but bound to effort.
18. *I heard him call upon Allah and say, beside the Black*
    Stone: "O my heart!
19. *Our night has quickly passed,*
    but the goal of my love has not passed!"

Ibn 'Imad said: "He died – may Allah have mercy on him!
– in the house of the Qadi Muhyi al-Din ibn al-Zaki and was
taken to Qasyûn [Damascus] and buried in the noble mound, one
of the groves of Paradise, and Allah knows best."[38]

Hand on earth...," and declared it *hasan* as a hadith of the Prophet ﷺ.
Ibn Qutayba in *Mukhtalaf al-Hadith* (1972 ed. p. 215) attributes it to
Ibn 'Abbas and relates a saying of 'A'isha that the Stone is the deposi-
tory of the covenant of souls with Allah. Its mention in the *Reliance of
the Traveller* (p. 853b) as "narrated by al-Hakim, who declared it
sahih, from 'Abd Allah ibn 'Amr," is incorrect.
[d] Multazam is the space between the Black Stone and the Ka'ba's door
(including the two) where prayers are surely answered.
[e] An allusion to the *kiswa* or black cloth covering the Ka'ba.
[38]Main sources: Hilmi, *al-Burhan al-Azhar*; Ibn 'Imad, *Shadharat al-
Dhahab* (5:190-202); al-Suyuti, *Tanbih al-Ghabi*.

Shaykh Muhyi al-Din Ibn 'Arabi
Islamic Doctrine
(*'AQÎDA AHL AL-ISLÂM*)[39]

Allah's Blessings and Peace Upon Allah's Messenger and Upon his Family and Companions

[*Al-Futuhat* §130] My faithful brethren– may Allah seal your lives and mine with goodness! – when I heard Allah's saying about His Prophet Hûd ﷺ, as the latter told his folk who had belied him and his apostleship: ❨**I call Allah to witness, and do you (too) bear witness, that I am innocent of (all) that you ascribe as partners (to Allah)**❩ (11:54), [I saw that] he called his folk to witness in his regard – although they belied him – that he was innocent of associating any partners to Allah, and that he positively confirmed His Oneness; and since he knew that Allah ﷻ will summon human beings before Him and

[39]From 'Uthman Yahya's edition of *al-Futuhat al-Makkiyya* (1:162-172), Part Three of "The Meccan Conquest," chapter entitled "Attachment Comprising the Essential Creed of All, Which is the Doctrine of the People of Islam Agreed To Without Examining the Proof Nor the Presentation of Evidence" *(Waslun Yatadammanu Mâ Yanbaghî an Yu'taqad 'alâ al-'Umûm wa Hiya 'Aqîdatu Ahl al-Islâmi Musallama-tan min Ghayri Nazarin ilâ Dalilin wa lâ ilâ Burhân).* Also quoted in full in Hilmi's *al-Burhan al-Azhar* (p. 69-77).

ask them about what he himself knew, either to exonerate or convict them, until every single witness bears witness;

[131]   And since it was related that the caller to prayer *(mu'adhdhin)* is witnessed to by every living and non-living thing as far as his voice can reach, and by everything and everyone that hears him; hence "The devil flees at the call to prayer, passing wind"⁴⁰ so that he will not hear the caller's call to prayer and then have to witness on the latter's behalf, thereby becoming one of those who contribute to the felicity of the one being witnessed to, whereas he is the absolute enemy and does not bear for us an iota of good – may Allah curse him!

[132]   Now, if the enemy himself is obliged to testify on your behalf to whatever you call him to witness regarding your own person, it is even more certain that your friend and beloved should testify on your behalf – for the latter shares your religion and belongs to your religious community – and it is more certain that you yourself should testify, in this world, for yourself, to Oneness *(al-wahdâniyya)* and Belief *(al-îmân)*.

The First Testimony of Faith

[133]   Therefore, O my brethren, O my beloved – may Allah be well pleased with you! – a weak slave calls upon you to witness, a poor one utterly dependent on His Lord in every glimpse of the eye, the author and maker of this book [*al-Futuhat al-Makkiyya* ("The Meccan Conquests")]; he calls you to testify in his regard, after calling Allah 🕮 to witness, His angels, and whoever is present with him and hears him among

---

⁴⁰Part of a hadith of the Prophet 🕮 narrated from Abu Hurayra by Bukhari and Muslim.

the believers, that he bears witness in word and in full conviction *(qawlan wa 'aqdan)* that:

[134]   Allah the Exalted is One God, without second in His divinity;

[135]   Transcendent above possessing a mate or a son;

[136]   Absolute owner [of all] *(mâlik)* without partner; absolute king *(malik)* without minister;

[137]   Creator *(sâni')* without any disposer of affairs *(mudabbir)* with Him;

[138]   Existing in Himself *(mawjûdun bî dhâtihi)*, without any dependence on, or need for an originator *(mûjid)* to originate Him. Rather, every existing thing other than Him, depends on Him and needs Him to exist. The whole universe exists through Him, and He alone can be said to exist in Himself.

[139]   There is no outset *(iftitâh)* to His existence nor end to His permanence. His existence is absolute and unconditioned.

[140]   He is subsistent in Himself *(qâ'imun binafsih)*: not as a spatially bounded substance *(jawhar mutahayyiz)* — for then place would be assigned to Him; nor as an accident *('arad)* — for then permanence would be impossible for Him; nor as a body *(jism)* — for then He would have a direction *(jiha)* and a front *(tilqâ')*.

[141]   He is transcendent *(muqaddasun)* above possessing directions *(jihât)* and regions *(aqtâr)*.

[142]   He can be seen with the hearts and the eyes, if He so wills.

[143]   He established Himself over His Throne just as He said and in the meaning that He intended; also, the Throne and everything else was established by Him *(bihi istawâ)*,[41] and ❴**unto Him belong the after (life), and the former**❵ (53:25).

[144]   He has no conceivable equivalent whatsoever *(laysa lahu mithlun ma'qûl)*, nor can minds represent Him. Time does not confine Him, nor place lift nor transport Him. Rather, He was when there was no place, and He is now as He ever was.[42]

[145]   He created fixity *(al-mutamakkin)* and place *(al-makân)*,[43] brought time into existence, and said: "I am the One, the Ever-Living" *(anâ al-Wâhid al-Hayy)*.[44] Preserving His creations in no way tires Him. Attributes which do not describe Him and are devised by creatures do not apply to Him.[45]

[146]   Exalted is He far above being indwelt by originated matters, or indwelling them, or that they be "after Him" or that He be "before them"! Rather, we say: "He was and there was

---

[41]Cf. al-Shibli in Ibn Jahbal's *Refutation of Ibn Taymiyya* §27 (published in full separately): "The Merciful exists from pre-eternity while the Throne was brought into being, and the Throne was established and made firm *(istawâ)* by the Merciful."

[42]See Appendix entitled "Allah is Now As He Ever Was" in our translation of Ibn 'Abd al-Salam's *al-Mulha fi I'tiqad Ahl al-Haqq*, published separately under the title *The Belief of the People of Truth.*

[43]Or: "He created place and all that takes place."

[44]I.e. I am in no need of any of you.

[45]*Lâ tarji'u ilayhi sifatun lam yakun 'alayhâ min sun'ati al-masnû'ât.* Ibn 'Arabi apparently allows inferred attributes which do describe Him, such as "The Far" (see §163 below and note) in contradiction of the general principle that the divine Names and Attributes are ordained and non-inferable (cf. Appendix entitled "Allah's Names and Attributes Are Ordained and Non-Inferable" in our translation of Ibn 'Abd al-Salam's *al-Mulha fi I'tiqad Ahl al-Haqq*).

nothing with him." For the words 'before' and 'after' are among the locutions of Time, which He invented.[46]

[147]   He is the Self-Sustaining Sustainer of All *(al-Qayyûm)* Who sleeps not, the All-Compelling Subduer *(al-Qahhâr)* Whom one resists not. ❨**There is nothing whatsoever like unto Him**❩ (42:11).

[148]   He created the Throne *(al-'arsh)* and made it the boundary *(hadd)* of *istiwâ'*, and He created the Footstool *(al-kursî)* and made it encompass the earth and the heavens.

[149]   The Sublimely Exalted *(al-'Alî)* contrived the Tablet and the Sublime Pen, making them bring about the inscription of His Knowledge concerning His creation until the Day of Determination and Verdict.

[150]   He contrived the entire universe without precedent. He created creation then caused what He created to wither.

[151]   He sent down the souls *(al-arwâh)* into the specters *(al-ashbâh)* as custodians, and made those soul-endowed specters deputies on earth.

[152]   He made subservient to us all that is in the heavens and the earth from Him, whereof not one atom moves except back to Him and because of Him.

---

[46]See our translation of Ibn Khafif's *Correct Islamic Doctrine* (published in full separately) §10: "In no way does He subsist in originated matters *(laysa bi mahall al-hawâdith)* nor they in Him." This is due to the mutually exclusive nature of contingency *(hudûth)* and incontingency *(qidam)*. The former refer to whatever is created, the latter to the beginningless and uncreated, "and the twain never meet."

[153]   He created everything without need for it, and no necessity drove Him to do so, but with His foreknowledge that He would create whatever He created.

[154]   ❨He is the First and the Last and the Manifest and the Hidden❩ (57:3), ❨and He is able to do all things❩ (5:120, 11:4, 30:50, 42:9, 57:2, 64:1, 67:1).

[155]   ❨He surrounds all things in knowledge❩ (65:12) ❨and He keeps count of all things❩ (72:28), ❨He knows the traitor of the eyes and that which the bosoms hide❩ (40:19). ❨Should He not know what He created? And He is the Subtle, the Aware❩ (67:14).

[156]   He knew all things before they came into existence, then He brought them into existence exactly as He knew them. He has known them without beginning to His knowledge, and such knowledge in no way becomes newer upon the renewal of origination *(tajaddud al-inshâ')*. He brought all things to perfection in His knowledge, then He established them firmly *(bi 'ilmihi atqana al-ashyâ'a fa ahkamahâ)*. Likewise, He has full knowledge of their smallest details *(juz'iyyât)* according to the consensus and complete agreement of the people of sound scrutiny.[47] ❨Knower of the invisible and the visible! and exalted be He over all that they ascribe as partners (unto Him)❩ (23:92).

[156—A]   ❨Doer of what He will❩ (85:16), He is therefore willing *(murîd)* for existent entities in the earthly and heavenly worlds. However, His power is without link to anything *(lam tata'allaq bi shay')* until He wills it.[48] Likewise, He does not will

---

[47]This is directed against the *Mu'tazila* and those affiliated with them.

[48]The notion of "linkage" *(ta'alluq)* between the preternal Attributes of Act and the acts pertaining to creation was expressed by some scholars as a distinction between two types of linkage *(ta'alluq)* to the act:

anything until He knows it. For it is impossible in the mind that He wills something of which He knows not, or that one who is endowed with the choice of not doing, should do what He does not want to do. Likewise, it is impossible that all these realities be attributed to one who is not living, and it is impossible that the Attributes subsist in other than an Entity described by them.

[157]   There is not in all existence any observance nor sin, any gain nor loss, any slave nor free man, any cold nor hot, any life nor death, any happening nor elapsing, any day nor night, any moderation nor inclination, any land nor sea, any even nor odd, any substance nor accident, any health nor sickness, any joy nor sadness, any soul nor specter, any darkness nor light, any earth nor heaven, any assembling nor disjoining, any plenty nor scarcity, any morning nor evening, any white nor black, any sleep nor wakefulness, any visible nor hidden, any moving nor still, any dry nor moist, any shell nor core, or any of all such mutually contrasting, variegated, or similar entities, except it is so willed by the Real – Exalted is He!

[158]   How could He not will it when it is He Who brought it into existence? And how could the one endowed with free will, bring into existence what He does not want? None can turn down His command, and none can dispute His decision.

[159]   ❨[He] gives sovereignty unto whom [He] will, and [He] withdraws sovereignty from whom [He] will. [He] exalts whom [He] will and [He] abases whom [He] will❩ (3:26). ❨[He] sends whom [He] will astray and guides whom [He] will❩ (7:155). Whatever Allah wants, comes into existence *(mâ shâ'a Allahu kân)*, and whatever He does not wish to be, does not come into existence *(mâ lam yasha' an yakûna lam yakun)*.

"beginninglessly potential" *(salûhî qadîm)* and "actualized in time" *(tanjîzî hâdith)*.

33

[160]   If all creatures convened to want something which Allah does not want them to want, they cannot want it. Or, if they convened to do something which Allah does not want to bring into existence – although they willed it whenever He wanted them to will it – they cannot do it; nor can they even be capable of doing it; nor does He enable them to.

[161]   Therefore, disbelief and belief, observance and sin, are all according to His desire *(mashî'a)*, His wisdom *(hikma)*, and His will *(irâda)*. And He –Glorified is He! – is described as possessing such will without beginning.

[162]   The universe is in oblivion and nonexistence, although firmly established in itself in [the divine] knowledge. Then He brought the universe into existence without reflection *(tafakkur)* nor deliberation *(tadabbur)* such as accompany ignorance or unawareness and would then presumably provide Him the know-ledge of what He knew not – greatly exalted and elevated is He above that! Rather, He brought it into existence on the basis of foreknowledge *(al-'ilm al-sâbiq)*, and the exact specification *(ta'yîn)* of transcendent, pre-existent will *(al-irâda al-munazzaha al-azaliyya)* determining just how it brought the universe into being with respect to time, place, forms, masses, and color. None exists exerting will, in reality, other than He. For He says: ❨And you will not, unless Allah wills❩ (76:30, 81:29).

[163]   Just as He knows, He determines *(kamâ 'alima fa ahkama)*; just as He wills, He details *(arâda fa khassasa)*; just as He foreordains, He brings into existence *(qaddara fa awjada)*. Likewise, He hears and sees whatever moves or stands still and whatever utters a sound in all creation, whether in the lowest world or the highest. Distance *(al-bu'd)* does not in any way hamper His hearing, for He is the Near *(al-Qarîb)*. Nor does

nearness *(al-qurb)* veil His sight, for He is the Far *(al-Ba'îd)*.[49]
He hears the discourse of the self in itself *(kalâm al-nafs fî al-*

---

[49]No such Attribute is established in the texts, but Ibn 'Arabi here
states it without contradiction of his own precept (§145, cf. §180) that
"Attributes which do not describe Him and are devised by creatures do
not apply to Him" since He uses "the Far" in the same way that some
have used the indefinite qualificative "Separate" *(bâ'in)* – likewise not
found in the Qur'an and Sunna – meaning "far and separate from creation," so that nearness in no way affects Him as it affects creatures. Al-
Tabari (in his *Tafsir* on verse 17:79) relates from some of the *Salaf* a
contrary position which states that Allah is not said to be "in contact
with," nor "separate from" anything. The latter is reminiscent of Abu
Nu'aym's narration from 'Ali in *Hilya al-Awliya'* (1997 ed. 1:114
#227): "How can even the most eloquent tongues describe Him Who
did not exist among things so that He could be said to be 'separate
from them' *(bâ'in)*? Rather, He is described without modality, and He
is ❴nearer to [man] than his jugular vein❵ (50:16)." Al-Bayhaqi
reports the Ash'ari position on the issue from Ibn Mahdi al-Tabari: The
Preternal One *(al-Qadîm)* is elevated over His Throne but neither
sitting on *(qâ'id)* nor standing on *(qâ'im)* nor in contact with *(mumâss)*,
nor separate from *(mubâyin)* the Throne – meaning separate in His Essence in the sense of physical separation or distance. For 'contact' and
its opposite 'separation,' 'standing' and its opposite 'sitting' are all the
characteristics of bodies *(ajsâm)*, whereas ❴Allah is One, Everlasting,
neither begetting nor begotten, and there is none like Him.❵ (112:1-
4) Therefore what is allowed for bodies is impermissible for Him." Al-
Bayhaqi, *al-Asma' wa al-Sifat* (Kawthari ed. p. 410-411; Hashidi ed.
2:308-309). This shows with remarkable clarity that those who made it
a categorical imperative to declare that "Allah is separate from
creation" went to excess, although their intention was to preclude
notions of indwelling. Examples of these well-founded excesses are
given by Ibn Khuzayma: "Whoever does not definitely confirm that
Allah established Himself over His Throne above His seven heavens,
separate *(bâ'in)* from His creation, he is a disbeliever who must be
summoned to repent" [in al-Dhahabi's *Mukhtasar al-'Uluw* (p. 225-
226)] and Sulayman ibn 'Abd Allah ibn Muhammad ibn 'Abd al-
Wahhab: "It is obligatory to declare that Allah is separate *(bâ'in)* from
His creation, established over His throne without modality or likeness
or examplarity" [in *al-Tawdih 'an Tawhid al-Khallaq fî Jawab Ahl al-
'Iraq* (1319/1901, p. 34, and new ed. al-Riyad: Dar Tibah, 1984)].

nafs), and the sound of the hidden contact upon its touch. He sees the very blackness in darkness, and water inside water. Neither admixture *(imtizâj)*, nor darkness, nor light veils Him,[50] **《and He is the Hearer, the Seer》** (42:11).

[164]   He 🕮 speaks, not after being previously silent nor following presumed tacitness, with a speech preternal and beginningless like the rest of His attributes, whether His knowledge, will, or power. He spoke to Musa 🕮. He named it [His speech] the divine Bestowal *(al-tanzîl)*, the Book of Psalms *(al-zabûr)*, the Torah, and the Evangel. [All this] without letters *(hurûf)*, sounds *(aswât)*, tones *(nagham)*, nor languages *(lughât)*. Rather, He is the Creator of sounds, letters, and languages.[51]

[165]   His speech is [spoken] without [the organs of] uvula and tongue, just as His hearing is without auditory meatus nor ears, His sight is without pupil nor eyelids, His will is without

---

[50]The Prophet 🕮 said: "His veil is light, and if He removed it, the glorifications *(subuhât)* of His face would burn everything His eyesight fell upon." Narrated from Abu Musa by Muslim, Ibn Majah, Ahmad, Abu 'Awana, Abu Dawud al-Tayalisi, Ibn Abi 'Asim, al-Ajurri, and al-Bayhaqi in *al-Asma' wa al-Sifat* (Kawthari ed. p. 180-181; Hashidi ed. 1:465-466 #392-394). Al-Bayhaqi said: The veil mentioned in this report – and others – refers to creatures for they are the ones who are veiled from Him by a veil He created in them. Allah said of the disbelievers: 《Nay, but surely on that day they will be covered from (the mercy of) their Lord》 (83:15). His saying: 'if He removed it' means if He lifted the veil from their eyes without empowering them to see Him, they would have been burnt and would have been unable to bear it." Al-Qurtubi in *al-Asna* (2:92) said: "If he had removed from them the veil, His majesty *(jalâl)*, awe *(hayba)*, and subjugation *(qahr)* would have caused everything His sight fell upon to disappear – from the Throne to the undersoil, for there is no end to His sight, and Allah knows best." Cf. Ibn Khafif's *'Aqida* §12: "Nor does He hide Himself *(istatara)* with anything created."
[51]See Ibn 'Abd al-Salam's refutation of those who claimed the preternality of letters and sounds in various passages of his *Mulha*.

cogitation *(qalb)* nor inner reflection *(janân)*, His knowledge is without compulsion *(idtirâr)* nor examination of any proof, His life is without the vapor which is caused in the cavity of the heart by the admixture of the elements. His Entity accepts neither increase nor decrease.

[166] Glorified, most glorified is He Who, from afar, comes near! To Him belongs tremendous majesty, surpassing goodness, magnificent generosity! Everything that is other than Him is but an outpouring of His munificence. His grace unfolds it and His justice folds it up again.

[167] He perfected the making of the universe and made it uniquely excellent *(akmala san'a al-'âlami wa abda'ahu)* when He brought it into existence and invented it. He has no partner in His domain *(milk)* nor joint disposer of affairs *(mudabbir)* in His dominion *(mulk)*.

[168] Whenever He shows favor He sends comfort and ease; and this is His kindness. Whenever He sends adversity He punishes; and this is His justice. In no way does He intrude upon another's domain so as to be attributed tyranny and injustice. Nor is anyone besides Him entitled to pass judgment on Him so that He could be attributed apprehension or fear from such. Everything other than Him is under the authority of His subjugation *(qahr)* and subject to the disposal of His will and His command.

[169] It is He that inspires with Godwariness or rebelliousness the souls of those who are legally responsible. It is He that disregards the transgressions of whomever He will, and holds to task whomever He will, both here and on the Day of Resurrection. His justice does not hold sway *(yahkum)* over His kindness nor does His kindness hold sway over His justice.

[170]   He brought forth the world as two handfuls *(qabdatayn)* to which He gave two levels *(manzilatayn)*, saying: "These are for Paradise, and I care not *(lâ ubâlî)*![52] Those are for Hellfire, and I care not!"[53] No-one raised the least objection at that time. One handful stands under the Names of His adversity *(balâ')*, and one stands under the Names of His favors *(âlâ')*.

[171]   If He wished that the whole universe be in felicity, it would be so; and [if He wished that it be] in misery, it would not have obtained the slightest degree of felicity. However, He did not wish it so, and it was exactly as He wished. Consequently,

---

[52]In *al-Nihaya*, entry *b-l-â*: "Al-Azhari said that a number of scholars glossed *ubâlî* as 'loathe' *(akrah)*." Meaning: "It adds nor subtracts nothing from My greatness."

[53]Narrated from Anas by Abu Ya'la with a chain of trustworthy narrators except for al-Hakam ibn Sinan al-Bahili who is weak, and by Ibn Marduyah; from 'Abd al-Rahman ibn Qatada al-Sulami by Ahmad and al-Hakim who declared it *sahîh*, and al-Dhahabi concurred; from Mu'adh ibn Jabal by Ahmad with a *munqati'* chain missing the Successor-link; from Abu Sa'id al-Khudri by al-Bazzar and Ibn Marduyah; from Ibn 'Umar by al-Bazzar and al-Tabarani; from a Companion named Abu 'Abd Allah by Ahmad in his *Musnad* with a sound chain according to Ibn Hajar in *al-Isaba* (7:258 #10198); from Abu Musa al-Ash'ari by al-Tabarani in *al-Kabir*; from Abu al-Darda' by al-Tabarani in *al-Kabir* and Ahmad with a sound chain in the *Musnad* according to al-Kattani. Also narrated, but without the words *lâ ubâlî*, from Abu Hurayra by al-Hakim al-Tirmidhi in *Nawadir al-Usul*; without mention of the handfuls, from 'Umar by Malik in *al-Muwatta'*, Ahmad, Abu Dawud, al-Tirmidhi *(hasan)*, al-Nasa'i, and others. Al-Suyuti in *al-Durr al-Manthur* under the verse **⟨And remember when your Lord brought forth from the Children of Adam, from their reins, their seed⟩** (7:172) cited other narrations to that effect from Abu Umama, Hisham ibn Hakim, and other Companions. Al-Fattani in *Tadhkira al-Mawdu'at* said its chain was "muddled" *(mudtarib al-isnâd)* because of great variations in it, which makes the narration *mutawâtir al-ma'na* or mass-narrated in its import – as opposed to its precise wording – as indicated by al-Kattani in *Nazm al-Mutanathir*, due to the great number of Companions that relate it.

people are either miserable or happy, here and on the Day of
Return. There is no possibility to change whatever the Preternal
One has decided. He has said, concerning prayer: "It is five
although it counts as fifty."[54] ❴**The sentence that comes from
Me cannot be changed, and I am in no wise a tyrant unto the
slaves**❵ (50:29) for My authority over the disposal of affairs in
My domain and the accomplishment of My volition in My
dominion.

[172]   All this is because of a reality that sights and insights
(al-absâr wa al-basâ'ir) are utterly unable to see, nor can mental
powers and minds stumble upon its knowledge except through a
divine bestowal and token of the All-Merciful's generosity
towards him whom He nourishes among His servants, and who
was fore-chosen for this at the time he was summoned to
witness. He then came to know – when He was given to know –
that the Godhead *(al-ulûha)* devised this allotment and that it is
one of the refinements of the One Who is without beginning.

[173]   Glory to Him besides Whom there is no effecter *(fâ'il)*,
nor any self-existent being *(mawjûd li nafsih)*! ❴**And Allah has
created you and what you make**❵ (37:95), ❴**He will not be
questioned as to what He does, but they will be questioned**❵

---

[54]Hadith *qudsi* within the narration of the Prophet's 喫 ascension: "The
day I created the heavens and the earth I made obligatory upon you and
upon your Community fifty prayers: therefore establish them, you and
your Community.... Let them be five prayers every day and night, and
let every prayer count as ten. That makes fifty prayers. This word of
Mine shall not be changed nor shall My Book be abrogated." See the
translation of Shaykh Muhammad ibn 'Alawi al-Maliki's his collated
text of the sound narrations of the Prophet's 喫 *isra'* and *mi'raj* entitled
al-Anwar al-Bahiyya min Isra' wa Mi'raj Khayr al-Bariyya translated
in full in Shaykh Muhammad Hisham Kabbani's *Encyclopedia of
Islamic Doctrine.*

(21:23), ❨Say—For Allah's is the final argument—Had He willed He could indeed have guided all of you❩ (6:149).[55]

---

[55]For §168-173 see also Ibn Khafif, *al-'Aqida al-Sahiha* §32-37: "[32] Allah is doer of what He will: [33] Injustice is not attributed to Him, [34] And He rules over His dominion as He will, without [anyone's entitlement to] objection whatsoever. [35] His decree is not revoked nor His judgment amended. [36] He brings near Him whomever He will without [need for] cause and He removes far from Him whomever He will without [need for] cause. [37] His will for His servants is the exact state they are in." The Ash'ari position is that Allah rewards and punishes without being obliged to do so by the actions of His servants ("Allah is doer of what He will"). He is free to place the disbeliever in Paradise and the believer in Hellfire without any injustice on His part ("Injustice is not attributed to Him"), since He owns all sovereignty over the heavens and the earth, and no one received any share or authority from Him to object to what He does. This is similar to par. 36 below. The evidence for this is in the verses: ❨Know you not that unto Allah belongs the Sovereignty of the heavens and the earth? He punishes whom He will, and forgives whom He will. Allah is Able to do all things❩ (5:40); ❨Say : Who then can do aught against Allah, if He had willed to destroy the Messiah son of Mary, and his mother and everyone on earth? Allah's is the Sovereignty of the heavens and the earth and all that is between them. He creates what He will. And Allah is Able to do all things❩ (5:17); ❨The sentence that comes from Me cannot be changed, and I am in no wise a tyrant unto the slaves❩ (50:29). At the same time it is obligatorily known that Allah does not take back His promise to reward those who believe and do good and punish evil-doers: ❨But as for those who believe and do good works We shall bring them into gardens underneath which rivers flow, wherein they will abide for ever. It is a promise from Allah in truth; and who can be more truthful than Allah in utterance?❩ (4:122). The scholars have described the former evidence as "based on reason" *(dalil 'aqli)* and the latter as "based on law" *(dalil shar'i),* noting that it is the latter which takes precedence over the former. Cf. al-Buti, *Kubra al-Yaqinat* (p. 149).

The Second Testimony of Faith

[174]   Just as I have called upon Allah and His angels, as well as all His creation and yourselves, to testify in my regard to my declaration of His oneness, likewise, I call upon Him – glorified is He! – and His angels, as well as all His creation and yourselves, to testify in my regard to my firm belief in the one He elected and chose from the very time he existed. That is: our master Muhammad ﷺ whom He sent to all people without exception, ❲a bearer of glad tidings and a warner❳ (2:119, 34:28, 35:24, 41:4) ❲And as a summoner unto Allah by His permission, and as a light-giving lamp❳ (33:46).

[175]   The Prophet ﷺ thus conveyed fully all that was revealed to him from his Lord, discharged His trust, and acted faithfully *(nasaha)* toward his Community. He stood, in his farewell Pilgrimage, before all those present among his followers, addressing and reminding them, deterring and cautioning them, giving them glad tidings and warning them, promising and threatening them. He showered them with rain and made them tremble with thunder. He did not address anyone specifically at the exclusion of others in his admonition. He did all this after permission from the One, the Everlasting ﷻ. Then he said: "Lo! Have I conveyed the message?" They replied: "You have conveyed the message, O Messenger of Allah!" So he said: "O Allah! Bear witness."[56]

[176]   Likewise, [I call upon all] to testify that I firmly believe in everything that the Prophet ﷺ brought – that which I know and that which I know not. Among the things which he brought is the decree that death comes at a time specified in Allah's

---

[56]Narrated from Abu Bakrah al-Thaqafi, Ibn 'Umar, Ibn Mas'ud, and Jabir by Bukhari, Muslim, Abu Dawud, Ibn Majah, Ahmad, and al-Darimi.

presence and that, come that time, it is not delayed. I, for my part, firmly believe this, without the slightest reservation nor doubt.

[177]   Just as I firmly believe and declare that the interrogation of the two examiners in the grave is true; the punishment in the grave and the raising of the bodies from the grave are both true; the review in Allah's presence is true; the Basin is true; the Balance is true; the flying *(tatâyur)* of individual Records in every direction is true;[57] the Bridge is true; Paradise is true; Hell-fire is true; **❰A host will be in the Garden, and a host of them in the Flame❱** (42:7) truly; the agony of that day is true for one group; as for another group, **❰the Supreme Horror will not grieve them❱** (21:103);[58]

-----

[57]The Prophet ﷺ was asked by 'A'isha – may Allah be well-pleased with her: "Will the beloved remember his beloved on the Day of Resurrection?" He replied: "On three occasions he will not: At the Balance until it either weighs for or against him; at the time the individual Records fly in every direction, so that he should be given his record either with the right hand or the left; and at the time a long neck comes out of the Fire, winding itself around them [at the Bridge over Hellfire]…" Narrated by Ahmad in his *Musnad* with a fair chain, 'Abd al-Razzaq, Ibn Abi Shayba, Ibn al-Mundhir, al-Hakim who stated it is *sahîh*, al-Ajurri in *al-Shari'a*, and 'Abd ibn Humayd in his *Musnad* as stated by al-Suyuti in *al-Durr al-Manthur*. Abu Dawud narrates it in his *Sunan* without mention of *tatâyur*.

[58]Another possible translation is: "the interrogation of the two examiners in the grave is real; the punishment in the grave and the rais-ing of the bodies from the grave are both real; the review in Allah's presence is real; the Basin is real; the Balance is real; the flying *(tatâyur)* of individual Records in every direction is real; the Bridge is real; Paradise is real; Hellfire is real; **❰A host will be in the Garden, and a host of them in the Flame❱** (42:7) really; the agony of that day is real for one group; as for another group, **❰the Supreme Horror will not grieve them❱** (21:103)." Cf. Ibn Khafif's *'Aqida* §83: "Paradise is true; Hellfire is true; Resurrection is true; the Rendering of Accounts is true; the Balance of Deeds is true; the Bridge [over the Fire] is true; the

[178]   The intercession of the angels, the Prophets, and the Believers, followed by the taking out of the Fire by the most Merciful of those who show mercy of anyone He wishes, is true; a group of the grave sinners among the Believers shall enter Hellfire and then exit it through intercession and gratification truly; eternal and everlasting world-without-end *(al-ta'bîd)* in the midst of the pleasures of Paradise is true for the Believers and those who affirm Oneness; eternal and everlasting world-without-end in the Fire for the dwellers of the Fire is true; and all that was announced by the Books and Messengers that came from Allah – whether one came to know it or not – is true.

[179]   This is my witness in my own regard, and it is the responsibility of each and every person that it reaches, to bring it forward if asked about it, whenever and wherever he may be.

Final Supplication

[180]   May Allah grant us and grant you the greatest benefit with this faith. May He make us adhere to it firmly at the time of journeying from this abode to the abode of true life. May He replace for us this abode with the abode of munificence and good pleasure. May He intervene between us and a dwelling with ⟨raiments of pitch⟩ (14:50). May He count us in the troop that take their record with the right hand and return from the Pond fully sated, those in whose favor the Balance weighs down and whose feet stand firm on the Bridge. Truly He is the Munificent *(al-Mun'im)*, the Giver of All Good *(al-Mihsân)*!

---

punishment of the grave is true; and the questioning of the angels Munkar and Nakîr is true."

[181] ❮All praise to Allah, Who has guided us to this. We could not truly have been led aright if Allah had not guided us. Verily the messengers of our Lord did bring the Truth!❯ (7:43).

Bibliography

Abu Nu'aym al-Asfahani. *Hilya al-Awliya' wa Tabaqat al-Asfiya'*. 12 vols. Ed. Mustafa 'Abd al-Qadir 'Ata. Beirut: Dar al-Kutub al-'Ilmiyya, 1997.

Al-Bayhaqi. *Al-Asma' wa al-Sifat*. Ed. Muhammad Zahid al-Kawthari. Beirut: Dar Ihya' al-Turath al-'Arabi, n.d. Reprint of the 1358/1939 Cairo edition.

-------. *Al-Asma' wa al-Sifat*. 2 vols. Ed. 'Abd Allah al-Hashidi. Riyad: Maktaba al-Sawadi, 1993.

Al-Buti. *Kubra al-Yaqinat al-Kawniyya*. Beirut and Damascus: Dar al-Fikr, 1997.

Al-Dhahabi. *Mizan al-I'tidal*. 4 vols. Ed. 'Ali Muhammad al-Bajawi. Beirut: Dar al-Ma'rifa, 1963.

-------. *Mukhtasar al-'Uluw li al-'Ali al-Ghaffar*. Ed. M. Nasir al-Din al-Albani. Beirut: al-Maktab al-Islami, 1991[2].

-------. *Al-Muqiza fi 'Ilm Mustalah al-Hadith*. Ed. 'Abd al-Fattah Abu Ghudda. Aleppo: Maktab al-Matbu'at al-Islamiyya, 1998[3].

Al-Fattani. *Tadhkira al-Mawdu'at*. Cairo: al-Matba'a al-Muniriyya, 1343/1924-1925.

Al-Hakim al-Tirmidhi. *Nawadir al-Usul*. Beirut: Dar Sadir, n.d. Repr. of Istanbul ed.

Al-Haytami, Ahmad. *Al-Fatawa al-Hadithiyya*. Cairo: Mustafa al-Baba al-Halabi, Repr. 1970, 1989.

Al-Haythami, Nur al-Din. *Majma' al-Zawa'id wa Manba' al-Fawa'id*. 3rd ed. 10 vols. Beirut: Dar al-Kitab al-'Arabi, 1982.

Hilmi. *Al-Burhan al-Azhar fi Manaqib al-Shaykh al-Akbar*. Cairo: Matba'a al-Sa'ada, 1326/1908.

Ibn 'Abd al-Salam. *Al-Ishara ila al-Ijaz fi Ba'd Anwa' al-Majaz*. Ed. 'Uthman Hilmi. <Bulaq?> Al-Matba'a al-'Amira, 1313/1895.

-------. *Al-Mulha fi I'tiqad Ahl al-Haqq*. In *Rasa'il al-Tawhid*. Ed. Iyad Khalid al-Tabba'. Beirut and Damascus: Dar al-Fikr, 1995. Also in Ibn al-Subki, *Tabaqat al-Shafi'iyya al-Kubra*, vol. 8 p. 219-229.

Ibn 'Arabi, Muhyi al-Din. *Al-Futuhat al-Makkiyya*. 1- vols. Eds. 'Uthman Yahya and Ibrahim Madkur. Cairo: al-Hay'a al-Masriyya al-'Amma li al-Kitab, 1972- .

Ibn al-Athir. *Al-Nihaya fi Gharib al-Athar*. 5 vols. Eds. Tahir Ahmad al-Zawi and Mahmud Muhammad al-Tabbakhi. Beirut: Dar al-Fikr, 1979.

Ibn Hajar. *Inba' al-Ghumr bi A'mar al-'Umr*. 4 vols. Ed. Hasan Habash. Cairo: Lajna Ihya' al-Turath al-Islami, Wizara al-Awqaf, 1994.

-------. *Al-Isaba fi Tamyiz al-Sahaba*. 8 vols. Calcutta, 1269/1853.

-------. *Lisan al-Mizan*. 7 vols. Hyderabad: Da'ira al-Ma'arif al-Nizamiyya, 1329/1911. Repr. Beirut: Mu'assassa al-A'lami, 1986.

Ibn 'Imad. *Shadharat al-Dhahab fi Akhbar Man Dhahab*. 8 vols. Beirut: Dar Ihya' al-Turath al-'Arabi, n.d.

Ibn Qayyim al-Jawziyya. *Al-Manar al-Munif fi al-Sahih wa al-Da'if*. 6th ed. Ed. 'Abd al-Fattah Abu Ghudda. Beirut: Dar al-Basha'ir al-Islamiyya; Aleppo: Maktab al-Matbu'at al-Islamiyya, 1994.

Ibn Taymiyya. *Majmu'a Fatawa Ibn Taymiyya*. 36 vols. Cairo, 1984.

Kabbani, Shaykh Muhammad Hisham. *Encyclopedia of Islamic Doctrine*. 7 vols. Moutain View: Al-Sunna Foundation of America, 1998.

Al-Kattani, al-Sayyid Muhammad ibn Ja'far. *Nazm al-Mutanathir fi al-Hadith al-Mutawatir*. Beirut: Dar al-Kutub al-'Ilmiyya, 1980.

Al-Kawthari, Muhammad Zahid. Ed. Al-Bayhaqi, Abu Bakr. *Al-Asma' wa al-Sifat*. Beirut: Dar Ihya' al-Turath al-'Arabi, n.d. Reprint of 1358/1939 Cairo edition.

Al-Nawawi. *Bustan al-'Arifin fi al-Zuhd wa al-Tasawwuf*. Beirut: Dar al-Kitab al-'Arabi, 1985.

Al-Qari. *Firr al-'Awn*. See *Risala Wahda al-Shuhud*.

-------. *Risala fi Wahda al-Shuhud*. Istanbul: Dar al-Ma'arif, 1294/1877.

Al-Qasimi. *Qawa'id al-Tahdith*. Beirut: Dar al-Kutub al-'Ilmiyya and Dar Ihya' al-Sunna al-Nabawiyya, n.d.

Al-Qurtubi. *Al-Asna fi Sharh Asma' Allah al-Husna*. 2 vols. Ed. Muhammad Hasan Jabal, Tariq Ahmad Muhammad, and Majdi Fathi al-Sayyid. Tanta: Dar al-Sahaba li al-Turath, 1995.

Al-Sakhawi, Muhammad ibn 'Abd al-Rahman. *Al-Daw' al-Lami' li Ahl al-Qarn al-Tasi'*. 12 vols. in 6. Ed. Muhammad Jamal al-Qasimi. 1313/1896. Repr. Beirut: Dar al-Jil, 1992.

Shatta, Ibrahim al-Dusuqi. *Sira al-Shaykh al-Kabir Abi 'Abd Allah Muhammad ibn Khafif al-Shirazi*. Cairo: al-Hay'a al-'Amma li Shu'un al-Matabi' al-Amiriyya, 1977.

Al-Suyuti, Jalal al-Din. *Al-Durr al-Manthur fi al-Tafsir al-Ma'thur*. 8 vols. Beirut: Dar al-Fikr, 1994.

-------. *Tanbih Al-Ghabi Fi Takhti'a* [or *Tanzih*] *Ibn 'Arabi*. Ed. 'Abd al-Rahman Hasan Mahmud. Cairo: Maktaba al-Adab, 1990.